LONDON'S UNDERGROUND

The World's Premier Underground System

11th EDITION

LONDON'S UNDERGROUND

The World's Premier Underground System

11th EDITION

John Glover

Ian Allan PUBLISHING

Front cover: *Swansong for the A stock; a standard 8-car formation arrives at Hillingdon, crossing the A40(M) bridge as it does so on 28 June 2008. This is not a formal park-and-ride station, but it is well connected by road and clearly has many users who park there for the day.* John Glover

Rear cover, upper: *The Northern line operates the largest fleet, of 106 trains, though the Central line has more vehicles as it uses 8-car instead of 6-car formations. This train of 1995 stock is getting ready to depart from the Edgware terminus on 7 May 2008.* John Glover

Rear cover, lower: *The Grand Union Canal viaduct is crossed by the Metropolitan's Watford branch less than a kilometre before reaching its terminus. The new route to Watford (High Street and Junction) will need to leave the existing railway before this point, and a new bridge will be built over the canal. A train of A stock crosses the Grand Union on 14 September 2008.* John Glover

Opposite title page: *The Northern Line extension from Golders Green to Edgware was built on the cheap, and there have been many subsidence problems. This view taken on 1 June 2009 looking north from Brent Cross platforms shows clearly the undulations, with a 1996 stock train for Morden via Bank approaching, and an Edgware-bound train receding into the distance.* John Glover

LONDON'S UNDERGROUND
John Glover

First published 1951
Second edition 1959
Third edition 1961
Fourth edition 1967
Fifth edition 1981
Sixth edition 1986
Seventh edition 1991
Eighth edition 1996
Ninth edition 1999
Tenth edition 2003
Eleventh edition 2010

ISBN 978 0 7110 3429 7

Published by Ian Allan Publishing Ltd

An imprint of Ian Allan Publishing Ltd,
Riverdene Business Park, Hersham, Surrey KT12 4RG

Printed by Ian Allan Printing Ltd
Riverdene Business Park, Hersham, Surrey KT12 4RG

Code: 1005/E

Visit the Ian Allan Publishing website at
www.ianallanpublishing.com

Distributed in the United States of America and Canada by BookMasters Distribution Services.

CONTENTS

INTRODUCTION

The Underground as we know it today has many reminders of its illustrious history, which now stretches back a century and a half. But the continuing major works of recent years carried out under the Public Private Partnership (PPP) contracts with, it must be said, their own share of difficulties, is beginning to have its effects. Major improvements to the infrastructure assets, mostly long overdue, are resulting in a cleaner and more welcoming environment.

Left: *A train of refurbished Piccadilly Line 1973 stock arrives at Ruislip with an eastbound working on 28 June 2008. These trains too will make their 40th anniversary before consignment to the breaker's yard. The reason for their introduction was the original line extension to Heathrow as long ago as 1977, for which the existing fleet of 1959 stock was deemed unsuitable.* John Glover

Below: *The Metropolitan was to fight a doughty battle to prevent it from becoming part of the London Passenger Transport Board in 1933, but to no avail. This is the company's coat of arms. It is intriguing to consider what might have happened had it been successful. Could today's Metropolitan main line be run as part of the Chiltern Railways franchise and be connected to the Widened Lines? It could then form the second northern outpost for Thameslink, rather than the Great Northern. Aylesbury to Brighton, anybody?* John Glover

To that might be added new trains, which are soon to be delivered in quantity. Those are only the most obvious results; much attention is being given also to matters such as track condition, drainage and signalling, matters which are of little concern to the average passenger until they go wrong. Asset reliability, system capacity and service regularity are major considerations. The aim is to make the Underground fit for purpose and to ensure that it stays that way.

That is just as well, since the relentless rise in the numbers travelling over recent years is putting enormous strain on the system. From a post-war high of 702 million passengers on the Underground in 1951, usage declined slowly over the next 20 years, reaching a low of 498 million in 1972. A sustained rise then took place, reaching 815 million in 1988/89, though it wasn't until 1997/98 that this was surpassed. From then onwards growth has occurred in nearly every year, and the 1bn mark was achieved for the first time in 2006/07.

All this is many years away from 1863, when the original section of the Metropolitan Railway was opened between Paddington and Farringdon. The system expanded slowly until the turn of the nineteenth century, when the advent of electric traction suddenly offered the opportunity to build deep-level tube railways. There followed a frenzied period of construction, and criss-crossing of the central area was completed by 1907.

The tubes vastly enhanced the travel opportunities in the built-up area, but by pushing out beyond it were also instrumental in the creation and nurturing of suburban London. This was particularly prevalent during the inter-war period.

Since then, much more limited expansion plans have seen the creation of more capacity in the centre with the Victoria and Jubilee lines, while their outwards expansion has been constrained to the relatively close-

in termini of Walthamstow Central, Brixton and Stratford. The other place to be newly served was Heathrow Airport, with the Piccadilly Line extended progressively to Terminals 1, 2, 3, Terminal 4 and Terminal 5.

This book offers a concise early history of the Underground and the various factors which have made it what it is. This is followed by a more detailed consideration of the present situation and the years to come. It is now a very busy urban railway indeed.

1

SUBSURFACE STEAM

London was settled by the Romans as it offered good drinking water and suitable locations for quays. Fifty kilometres or so up the Thames estuary, it also offered a degree of inland penetration by water, which was then far preferable to muddy tracks on land.

Thus the Thames became a major highway and, at the same time, a divider. The north bank with its better natural drainage was developed first. The growth of the population, one million in 1800, accelerated from the 1850s onwards and by 1900 it was over six million. London continued to spread outwards.

First railways established

The first main-line railways built for local traffic were the London & Greenwich, opened in 1836–8, and the London & Blackwall, opened from 1840. They were oriented towards passengers, as were subsequent lines constructed to the south and east of the city. Thus they contrasted with the main-line railways to the north and west, where short distance traffic was discouraged by few local stations and fewer trains. This led to the uneven development of the railway system, and later this provided business expansion opportunities for what became the Underground.

The Metropolitan

In 1855, a Parliamentary Select Committee considered how to combat growing road congestion. In his evidence, Charles Pearson, solicitor to the City of London, championed the cause of railways. He also had a social reforming instinct, and one of his aims was to clear the slums from the valley of the River Fleet and relocate their population in new purpose-built suburbs. They would then be able to travel cheaply to work by rail, using the special low workmen's fares which he had long advocated.

He was a leading light in the promotion of the

But why did those main-line railways stop at the edge of the central area? In the mid-1840s, the promotional boom surrounding railway building became intense. This nationwide phenomenon of the 'railway mania' was so strong that there were genuine fears that the capital would end up being over-run with railways.

This led to the setting up of a Royal Commission, which reported in 1846. The Commission recommended that the main-line railways should be excluded from central London, which resulted in their siting their terminals along today's Euston Road, and its continuations along City Road to the east and Marylebone Road to the west. In the south the barrier was to be the river.

With some exceptions, especially Charing Cross, that decision stood. The railways were therefore going to add to central London's traffic problems by disgorging passengers onto the road system at what were then the outskirts.

Metropolitan Railway, which was to '... encircle the Metropolis with a tunnel to be in communication with all the railway termini, without forcing the public to traverse the streets in order to arrive at their destination'.

Thus was evolved a plan for a steam-operated underground railway to run the 5.88 km between Farringdon Street and Bishop's Road, Paddington. It would serve as a link between the three main-line railway termini of Paddington, Euston and King's Cross. It also served St Pancras when that station opened in 1868.

Construction

Work began in 1860. The method of digging a trench for the trains and then roofing it over became known as cut-and-cover construction. Finding and diverting sewers, gas and water mains and drains was followed

Above: *This picture represents what might be termed the definitive view of the preserved Class 'A' 4-4-0T locomotive No. 23, outside the old power station at Neasden in January 1961. It is, once again, minus its protective cab. Did the Metropolitan really paint its steam locomotives in such brilliant colours and expect them to stay that way, given that they were destined to spend most of their days in somewhat insalubrious conditions underground? The late J. P. Mullett/ Colour-Rail (LT27)*

SUBSURFACE STEAM

by the excavation of vast openings in the streets 9m wide and 7.5m deep or more, to be lined with brickwork and roofed over, followed finally by the relaying of the streets for surface traffic.

According to *The Illustrated London News* in 1860, 'It is intended to run light trains at short intervals, and calling at perhaps alternate stations. All risk of collision will be avoided by telegraphing the arrival and departure of each train from station to station, so that there will always be an interval of at least one station between the trains.'

Traction

The means of traction was debated while the Bill was in Parliament. John Fowler, the Engineer, opted for a fireless locomotive, to be recharged with high-pressure steam at each terminus, and assisted with a firebrick heater on the locomotive itself to maintain a working pressure. This got the Bill enacted, but the technical problems proved altogether too much. Thus the Metropolitan opened for traffic on 10 January 1863, using conventional steam traction.

It had been a considerable feat to obtain finance and the costs of construction were inevitably huge in comparison with the length of the line. But an even greater potential hurdle must have been the attitude of the public to travelling in such conditions.

Opening

Private viewing days were laid on for William Gladstone as Prime Minister, Mrs Gladstone and other notables, who rode through the newly-built tunnels in decidedly un-statesmanlike open wagons. The formal opening was celebrated on 9 January 1863, with public services beginning the following day.

The Metropolitan was well-patronised from the start. With fares of up to 9d (3.75p) for a First Class return, as much as £850 was taken on the first day. Patronage was 9,500,000 in the first year and 12,000,000 in the second. It did not look back.

Closed carriages were used. This original section of

the Metropolitan was laid to mixed gauge, both standard at 1,435mm and the Great Western's broad gauge of 2,140mm. At first, the GWR supplied the motive power, rolling stock and personnel. Twenty two coke-burning 2-4-0Ts of Gooch design were fitted with condensing apparatus, to minimise the nuisance from atmospheric pollution. These were complemented by 45 eight-wheeled coaches of various origins, but all were lit by coal gas, as were the stations.

Great Western withdraws

The Metropolitan management were anxious to increase service frequency from the basic four trains an hour to cope with traffic running at 27,000 journeys daily, but the cautious Great Western objected to its effect on working costs. Only two months after opening, payments were being withheld.

Late in July 1863, Paddington issued an ultimatum that the GWR would cease all operations from 30 September, later advanced to 11 August. Furthermore, they would not sell the locomotives and rolling stock to the Metropolitan for it to run the service itself.

Both the Great Western and the City of London Corporation had put up substantial sums for the Metropolitan, the GWR seeing advantage in the access to the City which it otherwise had no hope of reaching. The Corporation wanted the removal of carts from the streets. Both it and the GWR were thus keen to see rail access to the new market at Smithfield.

Luckily for the Metropolitan, physical connections had been provided to the Great Northern company's lines. In concert with the London & North Western, the GNR managed to assemble sufficient rolling stock to work the services from 11 August using the standard gauge, which had so fortuitously been provided.

Service quality went downhill rapidly. On the first day alone, six trains were derailed due to misalignment of the hitherto unused standard gauge rails. One can only imagine the effects of something like that happening today! With an eye to the future, the Metropolitan hurriedly ordered locomotives and coaches of their own.

Locomotives

The Metropolitan's locomotives were outside-cylindered 4-4-0Ts built by Beyer Peacock & Co of Manchester. There was no cab roof, only a cab plate. When delivered, the engines were painted a bright green, with the typical Beyer Peacock fittings of polished brass domes and numbers on the copper capped chimneys. Each weighed just over 42 tons. Eventually orders for 44 of the outstandingly successful 'A' class were received,

The improved 'B' class followed, and ran to 22 locomotives with deliveries up to 1885. The Metropolitan replaced the green livery with a colour described as 'slightly darker than Midland Railway red' from 1885.

Above: The fine overall roof at Paddington (Circle and District Lines) looks down on two footbridges, the red paintwork of which sets off the whole impressive scene nicely. It is viewed here from the rear of the inner-rail platform on 24 June 2008. It was certainly designed to impress; the other similar roof that remains is at Notting Hill Gate, two stations away. John Glover

SUBSURFACE STEAM

Right: *The present South Kensington station entrance is an arcade, stretching from Pelham Street, seen here, through to Thurloe Street. It is 22 April 2009. As the decorative lettering above suggests, this was a joint project between the District and Metropolitan Railways. It now provides an entrance to the District, Circle and Piccadilly services, but the Metropolitan is a long way away. How the old signage can confuse, for those who stop long enough to think about it!*
John Glover

Right: *The facade of the District Railway station at Fulham Broadway, which was opened as Walham Green in 1880, is no longer in railway use. However, this and elements of the route thence to the platforms have been listed as being of architectural merit. The new station entrance is some distance to the east along the Fulham Road, and the platforms are entered at about their midpoint as opposed to the southern end. This view was taken on 1 June 2009.* John Glover

Ventilation

One of the biggest problems was to provide and maintain a supply of breathable air in tunnels and stations. The Metropolitan engines burned coke. This is clean, but gives off poisonous fumes, and after abortive trials with additional ventilation at the stations the railway went over to coal. This had the immediate result of an extremely smoky atmosphere.

The boring of 'blow holes' along the route covered by gratings in the roadways was the best solution that could be arranged.

The locomotives were fitted with condensing gear, which gave the driver a means of diverting exhaust steam from the chimney outlet into the water tanks.

Unfortunately, the blast on the fire was also much reduced and the power of the engine correspondingly impaired. However, maintaining schedules between closely spaced stations needed a pretty lively engine.

Conditions worsened as service frequency increased, and the replacement of the warmed condensing water with cold at the end of each journey was abandoned.

Coaching stock

The first of the new coaches was delivered by the Ashbury Railway Carriage Co in 1863. These catered for 1st, 2nd and 3rd classes, the furnishings decreasing in elegance accordingly, as did the space allotted per person. It seems a little incongruous that there should have been a 'No Smoking' rule applied impartially throughout, though this was later rescinded.

For the locomotive crews, the experience of driving steam locomotives underground, even with rather more openings to the sky than remain today, was not pleasant. Nevertheless, the locomotives performed a grand job, and one, No 23, has survived, to find a permanent resting place in the London Transport Museum.

The broad-gauge trains had disappeared for good from central London, and their rails were totally removed by 1873. It allowed station platforms to be widened, but even today some of the tunnel mouths appear to be rather wider than necessary.

Traffic

The Metropolitan was run first and foremost as a passenger railway and in 1868 it carried 28 million passengers. Workmen's trains were introduced at a fare of 1d (0.4p) per single journey, but the line remained peripheral to central London. Even so, it was outstandingly successful in attracting passengers and thus receipts, measured by its revenue yield per route km operated. This compared very well with its contemporaries.

Metropolitan District

Once the business was established, attitudes changed. The Metropolitan was murky and grimy, but that did

Left: The Metropolitan chose well when it ordered its 4-4-0T locomotives from Beyer Peacock. The earlier batches have no more than a very modest spectacle plate to shield the engine crew from the exhaust; this seemed to show a tremendous faith in the effectiveness of the condensing system. Here No. 46 stands at an unrecorded location, with its destination board reading New Cross. This was reached via the East London Line. The coaching stock displays the characteristic round-topped doors used by the Metropolitan, which minimised damage should they be opened in a tunnel section. The date is uncertain, but it may be shortly before electrification in 1905. F. Moore/ Author's collection

Left: Later on, with the Metropolitan extending its territory beyond and into the countryside, proper cabs became essential. Here is No. 23, the one which is preserved today, so fitted. Later as service stock No. L45, it survived until 1948. It came to rest first in the Museum of British Transport in the former bus garage in Clapham, moving then to Syon Park, and is now to be seen in the London Transport Museum in Covent Garden. Author's collection

SUBSURFACE STEAM

not deter the good people of west London from pressing for their own equivalent. At least the journey was in the warm and dry, and rather quicker and more pleasant than along streets bestrewn with horse dung.

A few years after the opening of the Metropolitan, the Metropolitan District started operations with an east-to-west route running through the heart of the capital. This was an entirely separate company. In the years to the end of the eighteenth century, each line was to carry out a programme of extension with the same object in view. This was to bring the suburbs and the underdeveloped country beyond into direct rail communication with central London.

The first section of the Metropolitan District Railway opened in 1868 between South Kensington and Westminster, a distance of 3.75km. Construction was not without difficulty; the Westbourne River had to be contained and carried over Sloane Square station in a conduit, and the company had to take special precautions not to undermine Westminster Abbey.

The Metropolitan District Railway followed the Metropolitan's example by securing 54 of the 'A' class locomotives. The principal (and important) difference was the Metropolitan's use of the automatic vacuum brake, whereas the District used the incompatible Westinghouse air brake.

The Metropolitan District used their locomotives until the end of steam traction in 1905, but the Metropolitan went on to purchase and build a number of other types of tank engines for general work.

Extensions

Concurrent developments saw what became known as the Inner Circle begin to take shape. The Metropolitan extended from a junction west of Edgware Road, with

a new line turning south through Notting Hill Gate to meet the Metropolitan District in an end-on junction at South Kensington. Environmental objections put paid to the original intention to run across Kensington Gardens and Hyde Park on the surface (as they certainly would have done today), and the present route was selected instead.

Working arrangements

For the first two and a half years, the whole line through to Westminster was worked by Metropolitan stock, under an agreement between the two companies, but in the meantime the District (as it quickly became known) extended its lines eastward under Victoria Embankment to Blackfriars. Bearing in mind the smoke problem, the later District Railway engineers built their line in open cutting wherever possible. The Embankment and this portion of the District were built together, the railway opening in May 1870 and the road six weeks later.

In the meantime, extension westward was contemplated. Projection to West Brompton over the District's own tracks took place in 1869, though the intended physical connection with the West London Extension Railway was never made. Kensington still lay on the western outskirts, and beyond it was practically open country, with places like Hammersmith and Chiswick still villages but growing rapidly. Extension became a fruitful proposition, District trains reaching Hammersmith in 1874.

In search of prosperity

The District pressed on westwards, reaching Richmond via the London & South Western Railway in

1877, and to Ealing Broadway in 1879. The West Brompton stub was pushed south to Putney Bridge in 1880, while arrangements were made to work the independently sponsored Hounslow branch from Acton Town in 1883. The District's last westward extension in the nineteenth century was over the Thames at Putney, to join up with the L&SWR to Wimbledon in 1889.

Meanwhile the Metropolitan had been driving steadily onwards, with an eastern extension to Moorgate in 1865. In the west a railway between Hammersmith Broadway and Bishops Road (Paddington) was opened in 1864, which became a joint Metropolitan and Great Western enterprise. Somewhat unwisely, the GWR had allowed this railway to cross their main-line on the level, replaced by a diveunder in 1878.

A service was also provided from Latimer Road to Kensington (Olympia), which ultimately gave access to the District at Earl's Court. The Metropolitan also gained access to Richmond from 1877 by a now-defunct connection at Hammersmith.

District revenues

The District's arrangements with the Metropolitan for that company to operate its trains meant that in return the Metropolitan received 55% of the receipts. However, this proportion was tied to a given service level, and if the District wanted more trains (as it did), it had to pay out more to the Metropolitan. Hoping to escape from what it considered to be an excessive payment to the other company, the District determined to work its own trains, and gave notice to that effect. It thus built for itself a depot at West Brompton, which later became the Engineers' Depot at Lillie Bridge.

Use of the Metropolitan's facilities would be avoided wherever possible, and for this reason the District created its own separate running lines westwards from South Kensington. The upshot was a prolonged 'who does what' battle on the 1872 Circle service between Mansion House and Moorgate; eventually the Metropolitan agreed that it would accept District trains providing half the Circle service on Metropolitan metals.

The District also worked its own lines. Although a solution had been found, further altercations followed on matters such as the division of receipts for bookings to the South Kensington exhibitions held annually on what is now the Imperial Institute site, and of which the 'Exhibition Subway' for pedestrians is a tangible reminder. The quarrels enriched nobody.

The District also provided decent rolling stock and this company too used coal gas lighting. The gas was produced at Lillie Bridge depot and transported at night in mobile containers to various points on the system, where the carriage cylinders could be recharged. The use of compressed oil-gas later became general in Britain.

Metropolitan extensions

While all this was going on, the Metropolitan began its long excursions into northwest London and the land beyond, a journey that was to take it eventually to Verney Junction in deepest Buckinghamshire and over 80km from Baker Street. The promoters of the Aylesbury & Buckingham Railway could hardly have imagined that their railway would one day become part of the London Underground system. Yet both the Aylesbury & Buckingham and the independent St John's Wood Railway, which built a single line from Baker Street to Swiss Cottage, were opened in 1868.

The Widened Lines

Meanwhile, the prospect of trains from the Great Northern and elsewhere converging on its tracks and disrupting its traffic had been exercising the Metropolitan, and it was decided to construct a second pair of tracks between King's Cross and Moorgate. East of King's Cross, the 'Widened Lines' dipped down through a second Clerkenwell Tunnel and then passing beneath the Metropolitan. When completed in 1869, a cross-London route was in place serving the Great Western, the Midland (via a connection to its new main-line north of St Pancras) and the London Chatham & Dover (by a spur from Blackfriars to Farringdon), as well as the Great Northern. All were thus enabled to reach the Smithfield meat market.

The Metropolitan reached the Great Eastern at Liverpool Street in 1875, building a little used and later removed connection with the main-line as well as its own station. Aldgate was reached in 1876.

For the time being, that was it, as far as the Inner Circle was concerned.

Completing the Circle

The Metropolitan was now under the control of the redoubtable Sir Edward Watkin, while the neighbouring District (which had generally been considered a natural business partner) was headed by James Staat Forbes. With conflicting railway interests in

Below: The Hammersmith branch from Paddington was more of a Great Western enterprise than that of the Metropolitan, though the latter soon became deeply involved. Most of it is elevated and the stations are basic in character. This is the entrance to Shepherd's Bush from the street, taken in 2007. This station has now been renamed Shepherd's Bush Market. John Glover

Kent, these two men were personal enemies. What price, therefore, the construction of an inordinately expensive piece of linking railway under the City between Aldgate and Mansion House, 1.82km long, which could only be worked satisfactorily in close co-operation?

Even without Watkin, relationships had been strained. Yet public clamour could not be resisted indefinitely. The necessary parliamentary powers were in existence, and eventually the work was completed on 6 October 1884.

The Act had laid statutory obligations on the companies to maintain the Circle line service once it had been established. But there were fundamental difficulties in running a railway without a terminus, such as how to recover from delays without the benefit of a layover. Steam locomotives also required servicing and their condensing water to be changed.

Eventually, a compromise of six Circle trains an hour instead of the eight intended enabled a workable result to be achieved. During busy parts of the day, the Metropolitan still managed to run an extra 13 trains an hour of its own along the northern side, a quite remarkable feat in the age of steam.

Other than the problems directly related to the use of steam traction, the same limitations remain today. How London Underground in recent times has attempted to resolve them is described later in this book.

Metropolitan main line

If the completion of the Inner Circle was something that had to be virtually forced out of the companies, the same could not be said for the Metropolitan's bid for main-line status. Sir Edward Watkin, Chairman from 1872 to 1894, also controlled the Manchester, Sheffield & Lincolnshire, the East London and South Eastern Railways, as well as having Channel Tunnel interests. It was not therefore altogether surprising to find him championing the Metropolitan as part of a great trunk railway from the Midlands and the north, across London to Dover, and thence to the continent.

By 1879 the Swiss Cottage appendage was extended to Willesden Green, and less than a year later to Harrow-on-the-Hill. At Neasden, a site was earmarked for workshops. The single track tunnel section from Baker Street to Finchley Road was doubled in 1882.

Pausing for breath, briefly, at Harrow, it was not until 1885 that Watkin got his railway to Pinner, followed by Rickmansworth in 1887. By now, the Metropolitan had a main-line 28km in length, which amounted to a very long country tail to wag the urban dog. From Rickmansworth began the unremitting climb for steam traction into the Chilterns at a ruling gradient of 0.95% (1 in 105). Though Aylesbury was the traffic objective and the company had the necessary powers to build the line, finance could not be raised and the railway was instead diverted to Chesham, 41km from Baker Street and reached in 1889.

Finally, the section from Chalfont & Latimer, which became the branch junction, to Amersham (38km) and Aylesbury (61km) was completed in 1892.

From Aylesbury, further possibilities arose. For this was the starting point of the Aylesbury & Buckingham line, which to Quainton Road provided a natural extension of the Metropolitan before turning north to Verney Junction on the Oxford-Bletchley railway. The A&BR's single line was promptly taken over by the Metropolitan, and doubled.

This allowed what was shortly to be renamed the Great Central Railway to press south and gain running powers over what were now Metropolitan tracks from Quainton Road. This was duly agreed, although separate running lines for Marylebone trains were constructed south from Harrow-on-the-Hill. This work was completed in 1899.

Wotton Tramway

There remained the oddity of the Wotton Tramway, or the Brill branch. This private railway was 10.5km long, with five intermediate stations and owned by the Duke of Buckingham. Trains took all of 1½ hours for the journey from Quainton Road, including stops. The line was completed to Brill by the summer of 1872. The first locomotives were a pair of thoroughly unconventional Aveling & Porter 0-4-0 geared machines.

The Metropolitan was pleased to work the railway and purchase the rolling stock. The company assumed control on 1 December 1899. It had already provided a new coach, much higher off the ground than the original offerings. Station platforms were raised, but as an economy measure they were altered at one end only, retaining the 1894 tramroad buildings at the old height.

The future is electric

By the mid-1890s, trams in London were conveying 280 million passengers per year. Horse buses were still supreme in central London, from which trams were excluded. There were around 10,000 (mostly) hansom cabs in use. At the end of the nineteenth century, steam operation on the Metropolitan and Metropolitan District Railways had nearly reached its zenith.

In a joint venture with the London, Tilbury & Southend Railway, the Whitechapel & Bow extension of the District line, with services to Barking and Upminster, remained to be completed. Services began in 1902, but operations beyond East Ham were not really established for another 30 years.

The Uxbridge branch of the Metropolitan from Harrow-on-the-Hill was built and steam trains began to work that line in 1904. This was a temporary expedient only; they were replaced by electric traction within six months.

That was the effective end of the expansion of what, collectively, are now known as the subsurface lines.

SUBSURFACE STEAM

Above: *The Metropolitan District purchased electric locomotives and used them as seen here in pairs on its through corridor express from Ealing (Broadway) to Southend via the London, Tilbury & Southend Railway. Of necessity, this was always a close relationship, due to the joint ownership and interworking at the eastern end of the District's operations. There needed to be a stop to change to steam traction and this could be at Whitechapel or somewhere further east, depending on the period and the extent of electrification. This service operated, with a range of variations, from 1910 to 1939. Author's collection*

Below: *The massive 'K' 2-6-4Ts formed a class of six locomotives built by Armstrong Whitworth & Co in 1925 from 'kits' produced at Woolwich Arsenal from a South Eastern & Chatham design. This accounts for their strong resemblance to the Maunsell 'N' class 2-6-0s of the Southern Railway, albeit that these were tender locomotives. Thus the 'K' class came about, with new side tanks, bunkers, cabs and rear bogies. This is No. 112. This class was too big to be used in the tunnels south of Finchley Road, but their main use was freight anyway. They were disposed of to the LNER in 1937. Colour-Rail (LT138)*

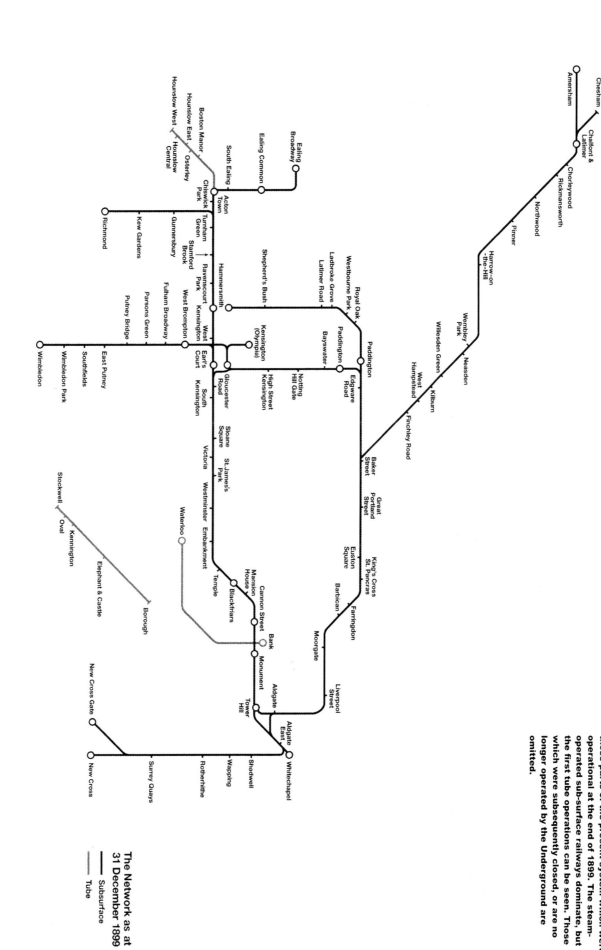

Growth of the system 1: This diagram shows those parts of the present system which were operational at the end of 1899. The steam-operated sub-surface railways dominate, but the first tube operations can be seen. Those which were subsequently closed, or are no longer operated by the Underground are omitted.

The Network as at 31 December 1899

Subsurface
Tube

Chesham
Amersham
Chalfont & Latimer
Chorleywood
Rickmansworth
Northwood
Pinner
Harrow-on-the-Hill
Wembley Park
Willesden Green
Kilburn
Neasden
West Hampstead
Finchley Road
Baker Street
Great Portland Street
Euston Square
King's Cross St. Pancras
Barbican
Farringdon
Moorgate
Liverpool Street
Aldgate
Aldgate East
Whitechapel
Shadwell
Wapping
Rotherhithe
Surrey Quays
New Cross
New Cross Gate
Tower Hill
Monument
Bank
Cannon Street
Mansion House
Blackfriars
Temple
Embankment
Westminster
St. James's Park
Victoria
Sloane Square
South Kensington
Gloucester Road
High Street Kensington
Notting Hill Gate
Bayswater
Edgware Road
Paddington
Royal Oak
Westbourne Park
Ladbroke Grove
Latimer Road
Shepherd's Bush
Kensington (Olympia)
Earl's Court
West Kensington
West Brompton
Fulham Broadway
Parsons Green
Putney Bridge
East Putney
Southfields
Wimbledon Park
Wimbledon
Hammersmith
Ravenscourt Park
Stamford Brook
Turnham Green
Gunnersbury
Kew Gardens
Richmond
Acton Town
Chiswick Park
South Ealing
Ealing Common
Ealing Broadway
Osterley
Boston Manor
Hounslow East
Hounslow Central
Hounslow West
Waterloo
Stockwell
Oval
Kennington
Elephant & Castle
Borough
Paddington

2

CLEAN ELECTRIC TRACTION

The pioneer driving of a 365-metre tunnel under the Thames between Wapping and Rotherhithe was undertaken by Sir Marc Brunel, and this was completed in 1843. The construction method was the first example of the tunnelling shield, forced through the earth and excavated from within. The tunnel walls were then lined with bricks.

The tunnel thus created was not intended to carry a railway, though that was the use to which it was put, much later. However, the basic methodology had been established.

Tower Subway

In 1869, Peter Barlow was engaged to drive a second Thames tunnel, between the Tower and Bermondsey. He improved on Brunel's method, using a circular shield and lined the tunnel instead with cast-iron segments. The Tower Subway was only 2.13m in diameter when completed, and this severely limited its usefulness. Barlow's shield was driven forward through the earth by levers and jacks, cutting into the clay. It progressed an average of 1.5 metres a day.

Both the method of tunnelling and the tunnel itself are notable in railway history, for Barlow's iron-lined tube was the first of its kind in the world. It opened on 2 August 1870. Since it also contained a small railway, this was also the very first tube railway. The single car seating 12 passengers was worked by cable. Bankruptcy caused the railway to close three months later and the lifts and the cable car were subsequently removed.

The Greathead shield

From these two beginnings evolved the Greathead shield. James Henry Greathead drove the tunnels for the King William Street–Stockwell tube railway in 1886, using a shield of his own design. It consisted of an iron cylinder divided into two by a bulkhead, with a rectangular hole for access to the workface.

It differed from Barlow's in so far as it was driven forward into the earth by hydraulic rams working at pressure. The rams pressed against the tunnel segments already fixed in place and forced the 3.65m diameter shield into the earth, enclosing a great core. Clay was removed from the face by hand, to a depth of about 600mm, with the spoil thrown back into the tunnel proper and removed by a small temporary railway. The excavated section of tunnel was then sprayed with liquid cement and a lining of cast iron rings

bolted together within the trailing end of the shield. As the shield moved forward, more cement was forced through the holes in the plates to fill the gap left between the lining and the clay, a process known as grouting.

The driving of tunnels required a great deal of precision if they were to meet accurately, since an error of only 2.5mm in sighting would throw the actual driving seriously out of alignment. Sufficient was now known to enable the whole of what would become the tube network to be cut accurately.

The shield was erected in position in a chamber formed by several rings of iron lining, and a short excavation made in the working face of the running tunnel. Provided the earth was soft enough for the purpose, piles were inserted between it and the edge of the shield, and a forward thrust of the shield drove the piles into the face and broke up the earth for easy removal.

Above: Building the tubes was by use of a shield driven forcibly into the earth, excavating from within, quickly lining the tunnel formed with cast iron segments, and of course disposing of the waste. Drainage, ventilation, tracklaying, provision of power supplies, signalling and communications all came later. This scene has been recreated in a cameo by the London Transport Museum. John Glover

Left: This view of an early City & South London Railway car well shows the gated arrangements for joining and alighting from the vehicle, and also the (very) limited windows through which the passengers could see the outside world. Inside, its occupants were advised by a notice to 'Wait until the train stops', presumably before leaving their seats to alight. This vehicle operated on the C&SLR for its whole life, from 1890 until 1924. London Transport Museum (U5285)

Right: Initially, the Central London Railway relied on electric locomotives to haul their trains. A series of problems, notably the vibration affecting properties above, soon saw their withdrawal and replacement with multiple-unit traction. No 12 survived for shunting duties, and is seen here in what is thought to be the yard at Acton Works in 1938 – despite still carrying its CLR markings. It was scrapped in 1942.
F. Moore/Author's collection

Above: On its corner site, Queensway is one of the original Central London Railway stations which opened in 1900. It has retained many of its original features, in an area much frequented by tourists. Within, platform access is still by lift. It is seen here on 1 June 2009. Whether or not its status as an operational Underground station is obvious is left to the reader to judge, but close inspection reveals two roundels. John Glover

Building the railway

Engineers may have to contend with more than clay or workable earth. They have encountered waterlogged sand or have had to tunnel below rivers and streams where normal methods would have quickly resulted in flooded workings. The general procedure is to construct airtight working chambers and compress the air within them, so that there is sufficient pressure to keep the water out.

Most of London's tubes have been driven through what is known as London clay which lies on top of the chalk and sand that once formed a sea bed. Roughly north of a line represented by Euston Road, the London clay comes to the surface, and stretches out as far as the chalk of the Chilterns. In central and southern districts of London, pockets of sand and gravel, often waterlogged, are found lying beneath layers of 'made ground' formed by the foundations of older London. Generally London rests on a very thick layer of clay which is anything up to 140 metres deep.

Even in Victorian London, it was clear that the 'cut-and-cover' method of railway construction was unacceptably disruptive to normal day-to-day living.

It was also not suitable for crossing the Thames. At the same time, the need to improve transport facilities within the central area became ever more pressing. An effective tunnelling method was therefore a prerequisite for the expansion which was to follow.

Another necessary technical development was the means of traction. Cable haulage had been used since the earliest days of railways, until it was supplanted by the steam locomotive. Could cables be used satisfactorily for underground railways?

City & South London

The 5km City & South London Railway was designed for cable haulage but the decision was then made to adopt electricity as the motive power. This promised to offer a higher average speed and, ultimately, to be a cheaper medium than cable.

Public services began on 18 December 1890. The trains were of three bogie trailer cars hauled by 11.8 tonne electric locomotives at an average speed of 18.5kph. This was a basic railway with little amenity value. It was designed for a purpose, without the constraints of compatibility with other systems. Its function was to take passengers from one station to another, avoiding the delays from road traffic.

This it did with remarkable success, and within three years of its opening was carrying 15,000 passengers each day. The coaches, appropriately nicknamed 'padded cells', were a mere 2.08m wide, designed for a tunnel purposely made as small as possible to reduce construction costs. Passengers sat on longitudinal benches, above which were tiny windows that were little more than ventilators. Electric lighting was provided, which was a luxury compared with the gas lights in the Metropolitan and District stock.

The two guards on each train were responsible for control of the gates at the ends of the cars and also for giving out the names of the stations. It seems that ridicule as much as anything else persuaded the company to build their future stock with larger windows; the fleet reached 170 cars by 1908.

Locomotives

A fleet of (eventually) 52 locomotives was in service by 1901 from a number of manufacturers. These were minute four-wheeled machines, being only 4.27m long, 1.98m wide and 2.59m high. The driving cabs extended from front to rear, with the driver facing sideways though he had an assistant. All were driven by a pair of modest 37kw motors.

They were little more than electric motors on wheels, but their basic and highly practical design was rewarded by many years of hard work, hauling 40-tonne trains at speeds of up to 40kph.

The running line was never less than 13.5m below ground. Workshops and depot were on the surface, reached by an amazingly steep 29% (1 in 3½) inclined ramp at Stockwell. Later, a hoist was installed. The running lines were in their own separate tunnels of 3.1m diameter north of the Elephant and 3.2m to the south. This reflected the greater speed planned with cable haulage on the southern section and which would increase the sideways sway of the trains.

At the termini, the running tunnels merged into one larger elliptical tunnel. Locomotives had to be stepped back so that they could return on the front end of the subsequent train. Coupling and uncoupling were jobs for the driver's assistant. The stations and passages were entirely lined with white tiles, except where covered with advertisements.

All the original stations had Armstrong hydraulic lifts for passenger access, which lasted for up to 15 years; later stations were equipped with electric ones.

Power was taken from the company's own power house at Stockwell.

System expansion

Popularity had the result that capacity became a real problem and the signalling system was modified to allow more trains to be run. A replacement was needed for the small King William Street terminus and the line was diverted to Bank, opened in 1900. Later extensions took it in stages south to Clapham Common and north to Euston. This final section opened in 1907.

It became obvious that the C&SLR needed reconstruction in terms of new signalling, the enlargement of the stations to take longer trains, and the reconstruction of the tunnels to what became the standard diameter of 3.56m. Such work was well beyond the company's financial capabilities, and an agreement was sought with the Underground Electric Railways Company of London which by then controlled most of the other underground lines. Consequently, control passed to the UERL in 1913, although the expansion work did not begin for a further nine years.

Waterloo & City

The completion of the Circle in 1882 had resulted in the linking of all the main-line railway termini that were not within walking distance of the City; all, that is, except Waterloo. This was a serious shortcoming as far as the London & South Western Railway was concerned, and to remedy it they promoted a direct tube link using the newly developed technology and backed with that Company's substantial resources.

The second tube railway in the capital was opened in 1898. Completely self-contained and with the two stations at Waterloo and Bank only, this modest

Left: *The extension of the Central Line beyond Shepherd's Bush to the original Wood Lane terminus in 1908 always left much to be desired. Because of the original depot connections, the terminal loop was negotiated in an anti-clockwise direction. When extension works to cater for six-car trains were carried out in 1928, the platform would have fouled the depot exit track (right). That on the left is the line from Shepherd's Bush. Thus the platform extension was made moveable, a feature used when depot access was needed. It was interlocked with the signalling. The picture is undated. Author's collection*

Right: *The Great Northern & City opened its line to Moorgate in 1904. The service was cut back from Finsbury Park to Drayton Park in 1964. This was to allow conversion of one of the platform tunnels, seen here in June 1970, for use by southbound Victoria Line services. The finishes are different from other stations on this line, and the tunnel diameter rather greater than is usual with tube stock. Also noticeable is the pronounced hump in the platform, where an up gradient into the station turns into a downward one.* John Glover

Right: *The Great Northern & City opened its line to Moorgate in 1904. The service was cut back from Finsbury Park to Drayton Park in 1964. This was to allow conversion of one of the platform tunnels, seen here in June 1970, for use by southbound Victoria Line services. The finishes are different from other stations on this line, and the tunnel diameter rather greater than is usual with tube stock. Also noticeable is the pronounced hump in the platform, where an up gradient into the station turns into a downward one.* John Glover

Right: *South Kensington station for what became the Piccadilly was built alongside the subsurface premises. Later, the two were merged, and the Leslie Green building became redundant from the passengers' point of view. It does, however, still stand and carries the station name. This view of the exterior was taken on 22 April 2009.* John Glover

2.03km line crosses beneath the Thames near Blackfriars Bridge. An inclined tunnel formed the exit from the system at Bank, and remained thus for the next 62 years. The line's power station and sidings were at Waterloo, where a hoist brought cars to the surface.

This was the first tube line to use rolling stock with motor cars instead of locomotives and the bodywork of the 22 cars was built in America with electrical equipment from Siemens. The vehicles were assembled at Eastleigh. The open saloons had seats formed of perforated plywood, without any upholstery. To reduce the cost of operation during the day when traffic was light, five additional single-unit motor cars were supplied by Dick, Kerr of Preston the following year.

Current collection was from a centre conductor rail, and the trains were formed of a pair of motor cars with two intermediate trailers. Eight power cables ran along the roofs of the trailers to connect the power cars, a feature which was not allowed on any other tube railway. Commendably, all electrical gear was arranged so that it did not reduce the length of the vehicles which

was available for passenger use, although the truly massive motor bogies with their 838mm diameter wheels had a raised floor level above them.

A Siemens shunting locomotive was provided to work in the sidings at Waterloo.

Historically, the line never had any formal connection with the Underground railways or London Transport. The Waterloo & City remained with the LSWR and their successors until it passed to London Underground in 1994. The original system proved to be sound both in design and construction, and few changes were made until the next generation of rolling stock was acquired in 1940.

Central London Railway

The Central London Railway, at 9.14km in length, became the core of today's Central line in 1900. It ran through the heart of London in an area which until then had not seen a railway of any kind.

Its route was from Bank and westwards in a straight line to Shepherd's Bush. There were 11 intermediate stations. It was decided not to use the open island platform arrangement favoured by the C&SLR and instead to separate the twin tubes widely enough to allow a platform for each direction, joined to its neighbour by cross passages. Where the streets were narrow, one tube was placed directly above the other to take advantage of the free wayleaves thus obtained. In the anxiety not to incur compensation costs as a result of undermining buildings, some ferocious curves were introduced between St Paul's and Bank. This has proved to be a lasting nuisance, particularly at Bank station where the train-to-platform gap can be excessive.

The platforms were 99 metres long and the stations were finished with white tiling. Electric arc lamps illuminated the platforms, which were reached by electric lifts, offering an altogether more attractive environment than the C&SLR. This superiority was continued in the 170 cars, which were built by Ashbury and Brush to take full advantage of the increased tunnel size. Although the intention had been to use the recommended 3.50m diameter tunnels, a later decision not to line the cast-iron segments of the tubes resulted in an effective diameter of 3.56m, which became the standard.

The tunnels themselves were made to dip on leaving the stations and to rise on approach to them. This was to help decelerate the approaching train and to accelerate it on leaving. A falling gradient of about 3.3% (1 in 30) results in a saving in current consumption, and conversely the rising gradient, which is made rather less acute, results in an economy on brake wear.

The Central London Railway was opened on 27 June 1900 by Prince Edward, with public services starting on 30 July. It deserved to be, and was, an instant success. Besides business traffic, the line managed to tap the theatre, shopping and hotel areas of the West End as well. It attracted over 40 million passengers in its first full year of operation in 1901. This was eight times the numbers generated by the City & South London after a similar period.

It was a tremendous improvement on the Metropolitan, still wedded to steam. However, the Central London too had its difficulties.

For a start, the locomotives took up valuable platform space but, more seriously, they gave rise to complaints of vibration. Fortunately, a technical solution was at hand thanks to the work of Frank J. Sprague in Chicago. Sprague is credited with the invention of multiple-unit working, whereby a single master-controller uses a low-voltage circuit to achieve simultaneous control of all the traction motors in a train. This overcomes concerns about the wisdom of allowing high current traction power to be transferred by cable along its length.

Successful experimentation led to an order for 64 new motor cars, and these were delivered in 1903 from the Metropolitan Railway Carriage & Wagon Co and the Birmingham Railway Carriage & Wagon Co. However, much valuable passenger space was still taken up by the control equipment and switchgear. Another hugely worthwhile outcome was the ability to run trains at two-minute intervals (30 trains per hour) if required, thanks to the quick turnrounds which could be achieved. The electric locomotives were scrapped.

CLR expansion

The first extension to the Central London Railway was opened in 1908 to serve the Franco-British Exhibition at White City. In view of the existing depot connections, the terminal loop provided was negotiated in an anticlockwise direction, with a single platform at Wood Lane. This introduced some

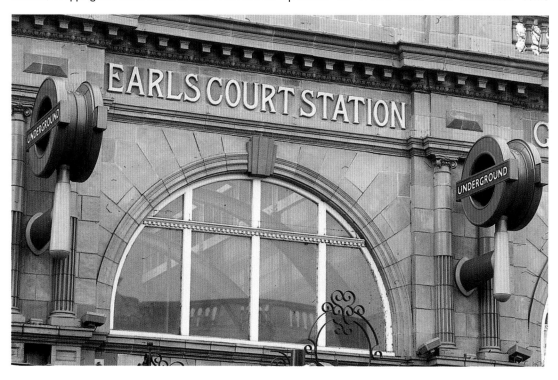

Left: *This is the eastern end frontage to Earl's Court station which was opened in 1906. It was designed by Harry Warton Ford, but the hand of Leslie Green can be seen in the half-round windows. This photograph was taken on 9 March 2008.* John Glover

operating and technical problems, since cars were 'handed' depending on the direction they faced and they could now be turned in the course of their journeys. The importance of 'handing' lies in the electrical and air pipe connections made between cars, since unless these are arranged symmetrically about the centre (and are thus expensively duplicated), a car to be coupled to another cannot be reversed. The penalty for not providing full reversibility is the constraint in limiting what may be coupled to what.

At the eastern end, Liverpool Street was reached in 1912.

Motor bus competition ate into receipts from 1905 onwards, and the Central London Railway was drawn inexorably into closer co-operation with the Underground Group, under whose control it fell in 1913. Commercially, it was known by the nickname 'Twopenny Tube' long after graduated fares were adopted. From 1911 the company decided to carry parcels in compartments set aside on the trains, sorted en route by a porter and then delivered by messenger boys on tricycles.

Great Northern & City

By far the most massive of all tube construction in London resulted in the building of the big 4.88m diameter bores of the Great Northern & City Railway, between Finsbury Park and Moorgate. The original intention was to allow Great Northern trains to reach the City direct via a connection at Drayton Park, but this ambition was frustrated for over 70 years.

This 5.6km line was built by using an extra-powerful Greathead shield, but as the shield progressed the lower cast-iron segments were removed and replaced by a blue brick invert as an economy. It was the only economy which was practised, since the stations were built a full 128 metres long (and 137 metres at the termini), in the fond hope that one day they would be needed by Great Northern trains. They appeared immense and deserted, as indeed they mostly were during what was then termed the slack hours.

The line was electrified from the outset using multiple-units on the Sprague principle; it opened in 1904. Both positive and negative conductor rails were placed 254mm outside the running rails and 51mm above them. For the first time the running rails were used to carry track circuits in the modern sense and to provide automatic signalling using treadles. The unique conductor rail arrangement remained in use until the original cars were replaced in 1939. It was then converted to Underground standard.

Thirty-two motor and 44 trailer cars were built for the service by Brush and Dick, Kerr. Trains of six cars operated in the peak, and two cars at other times. The line had its own power station near Essex Road.

In 1913 the line was acquired by the Metropolitan Railway, with which it never had any physical connections. The new owners promptly abandoned the GN&CR power station and provided their own supplies from Neasden.

Success in the promotion of underground railways was far from a foregone conclusion, and many lesser schemes fell by the wayside. But there were some deserving ideas. The common denominator was a lack of financial backing, but the industry was to find this in the person of an American banker and stockbroker.

Below: The station forecourt at Golders Green has a large bus station in front of it; the station buildings are seen here on 1 June 2009. When the station was opened in 1907 this was just a rural crossroads; housing development and a local shopping centre soon arrived and buses (also once trams and then trolleybuses) were used to bring people in from a wide catchment area. This was a pattern to be repeated later, notably at the other end of the Northern line at Morden and also at Edgware. John Glover

Left: *Tube stock long had the problem of needing to use part of the car-body space for equipment; it was not until the mid-1930s that a way was found of stowing this underneath the floor. In any event, the large bogies required the floor to be upswept behind the driving cab. The tops of the wheels of the trailing bogie were accommodated beneath the end seats in the passenger saloon, a situation which continues today. This car was clearly intended for the Charing Cross, Euston and Hampstead Railway, a constituent of today's Northern line. Highgate was the original name for today's Archway. Locomotive Publishing Co/ Ian Allan Library*

Left: *Hampstead is a typical Leslie Green-brand station as featured widely on the Yerkes tubes, with the arches surrounding the ox-blood tiles. As elsewhere, the separate exit to the street (on the left) is no longer used, as by funnelling passengers incoming and exiting through one barrier line, staff economies can be made. This bus is on route 46 from Lancaster Gate via Swiss Cottage, and it may be noted that all Underground stations are now served by a local bus service. Buses can also provide useful links between Underground lines; but they never seem to be advertised as such. It is 1 June 2009. John Glover*

The Yerkes tubes

Charles Tyson Yerkes was born in 1837, and spent many years in making dubious fortunes for himself out of tram companies. He came to London, backed by a new and unwary group of US investors.

Underground railway expansion in London was faltering. There were a number of other tube railway schemes which had secured their Acts, but construction work was advancing slowly at best. For the Metropolitan and the Metropolitan District, the question of electrification or not, and then on what system, was looming.

Yerkes was quickly involved in the District, confirmed by his taking a controlling stake in that company in 1901. His interests quickly expanded. The Metropolitan District Electric Traction Co (MDET) was created for the purpose of electrifying that railway and the building of the power station at Lots Road, Chelsea, to supply it. Within a year the Company had bought out the Charing Cross, Euston & Hampstead Railway interests (a constituent of the Northern line), the Brompton & Piccadilly Circus and the Great Northern & Strand (combined and enhanced to become today's Piccadilly) and the partially constructed Baker Street & Waterloo. In 1902 the MDET was

Right: *Access from the lower lift landings to the steps to the platforms at many Underground stations lay via a route which cut across the top of the station tunnel. This general view at Hampstead shows the tiling on the walls, which is typical of the Leslie Green approach and the period generally. The date is 1 June 2009.*
John Glover

revamped as the Underground Electric Railway Company of London Ltd (UERL). Yerkes was its Chairman, and although some variations to schemes already authorised were approved, no more underground railway proposals outside the UERL empire survived to be built.

Through Edgar Speyer, it proved possible for Yerkes and the UERL to raise the capital to build them. Thus central London gained a network of underground lines about 24 metres below ground level, which was to remain in its 1907 form for a further 60 years. Yerkes died in 1905 before any of his tubes were opened, while George Gibb of the North Eastern Railway was brought into manage the undertaking.

The Baker Street and Waterloo Railway, or Bakerloo, was opened to traffic in March 1906 between Baker Street and what is now Lambeth North. By the end of 1907 the Piccadilly and Hampstead tubes had also come into being. Using current station names, the Yerkes tube lines therefore were:
- Edgware Road and Elephant & Castle
- Finsbury Park and Hammersmith, with a branch from Holborn to Aldwych
- Golders Green and Charing Cross, with a branch from Camden Town to Archway.

Buildings and equipment

Common ownership had brought a number of common features, one of the most distinctive being the stations. Designed by Leslie Green, many of the 'ox-blood' coloured tiles cladding steel-framed buildings, sometimes with further offices above, were designed to catch the attention of passers-by. At platform level, a common approach saw tiles on the walls spelling out the station name in large letters, while the tiled surrounds were colour-coded to aid station recognition. All platforms were constructed of concrete slabs.

On the track itself, the rails were carried on sleepers of Jarrah and Karri wood, which is practically non-combustible.

The Yerkes tube lines were all fitted with automatic signalling which relied on track circuits, with the additional refinement of the automatic train stop.

With a requirement for nearly 500 tube-stock cars in the space of a couple of years, many manufacturers were involved, though there was little enough British input. They were sourced from the United States, France and Hungary. All cars had steel body shells.

The spring-loaded 'dead man's handle' was fitted and this enabled the trains to be worked in safety by a motorman only, without an assistant. The passenger 'gate stock', as it was called, required staffing by a man between each pair of cars to open the twin saloon doors and the gates onto the platforms. A single-stroke bell was provided on each car platform, operated from the platform at the other end of the car. When the train was ready to start, the guard at the rear passed a signal to the motorman via each of the gatemen en route.

The cars were all compatible with each other. Each was 15.2m long, but a section of the body of the motor cars was taken up with a control compartment. Doors were provided at the ends of the cars only, leading to the platforms, but the interiors were already adopting transverse seats in the centre with longitudinal seats over the bogies in the ends, which would be familiar to succeeding generations.

Depots were provided at London Road for the Bakerloo, Lillie Bridge for the Piccadilly and at Golders Green for the Hampstead tube.

Competition and reorganisation

Competition from the electric tramways and motor buses in the latter part of the decade depressed the fortunes of all the underground railways. Further American involvement came with the recruitment of Albert Henry Stanley. He came to London to support Gibb, and ultimately to succeed him. Later created Lord Ashfield, he was destined to become the future driving force of London Transport. Here, as Chairman, he was to combine the disciplines of commercial management with public accountability, and an awareness of the social benefits that a co-ordinated public transport system could bring.

Financially, the situation was slowly restored, helped on its way by the establishment of the London Traffic Conference (or operator cartel). Fares were gradually forced up to avoid ruinous competition, and the companies agreed to a joint marketing policy with the use of the word 'Underground'. Thus Frank Pick entered the scene; from that time on, the contribution of good design was to be exploited wherever possible.

In 1910 the Yerkes tubes were formally merged. Now under the guidance of Stanley, the UERL began to swallow up bus and tramway companies. The UERL became known as the 'Combine', and co-ordination with the development of through fares became the order of the day. Of the underground railways, by 1912 only the Metropolitan with its Great Northern & City appendage stood apart, as did the Waterloo & City.

Consolidation

An early result of the Combine was the promotion of a terminal loop for the Hampstead tube. Projection (present names) of the Northern line southwards beyond Charing Cross in a terminal loop running under the Thames and calling at what is now the northbound platform at Embankment offered interchange with both the District and Bakerloo. It was opened in 1914 as part of a rebuilding scheme for the station.

It followed a projection of the Bakerloo to Paddington in 1913. The London & North Western Railway provided the capital needed for a further extension of the Bakerloo to Queen's Park. This was to enable an integrated service to be offered with its own electric trains using the 'New Line', built to tap the suburban potential of local services out as far as Watford.

Bakerloo trains were extended as electrification permitted, reaching Watford Junction in 1917. This was the first time that a tube line had come into direct physical contact with a main-line railway, and this raised some floor height compatibility problems at station platforms. The new Joint Stock compromised and the floor level of the new trains, which were finished in LNWR livery, was 1,143mm higher.

Incidentally, when the same problem arose later because of joint running between the District and Piccadilly lines, the track was raised so that the difference was spread between the two floor heights.

The physical scale of what was being achieved was quite breathtaking. In 1863 the Metropolitan Railway started operation with a mere seven stations. By 1902, the number of stations on what was to become London Underground had expanded to 97, and by 1911 there were as many as 155. Over the same period, the route km rose from 5.88km (1863) to 109km (1902) and 174km (1911).

Although not all of it was below ground level, this equated to the building of well over three km of railway and three stations in each and every year for almost half a century.

Left: The Yerkes tube stations all had a likeness at platform level, as well as on the surface. This is Caledonian Road, one of the more lightly used stations on the Piccadilly Line, on 7 November 1948. Fluorescent strip lighting has arrived, but the Next Train indicator doesn't admit to there ever being one. The cabinet with the then fire precautions can be seen on the left. The picture indicates business as usual. Author's collection

Above: *The Bakerloo managed a remarkable entrance to Maida Vale station, opened in 1915. Above the stairs leading down to the subsurface ticket hall, passengers are met with a mosaic at high level, which today seems as bright as it ever was. An identical mosaic in the other corner greets passengers climbing the stairs. It is 7 May 2008. John Glover*

Below: *The use by the Bakerloo of LNWR metals from Queen's Park to Watford Junction required adaptations by both parties. Tube trains were extended north from Queen's Park in 1916. This is one of the borrowed Central London Railway trains used to inaugurate services, as the new joint stock was not ready. This train is seen between Harrow & Wealdstone and Kenton alongside a strangely deserted West Coast Main Line. Differences in platform heights meant that passengers had to negotiate a 250mm step at all the LNW stations. Locomotive Publishing Co/Ian Allan Library*

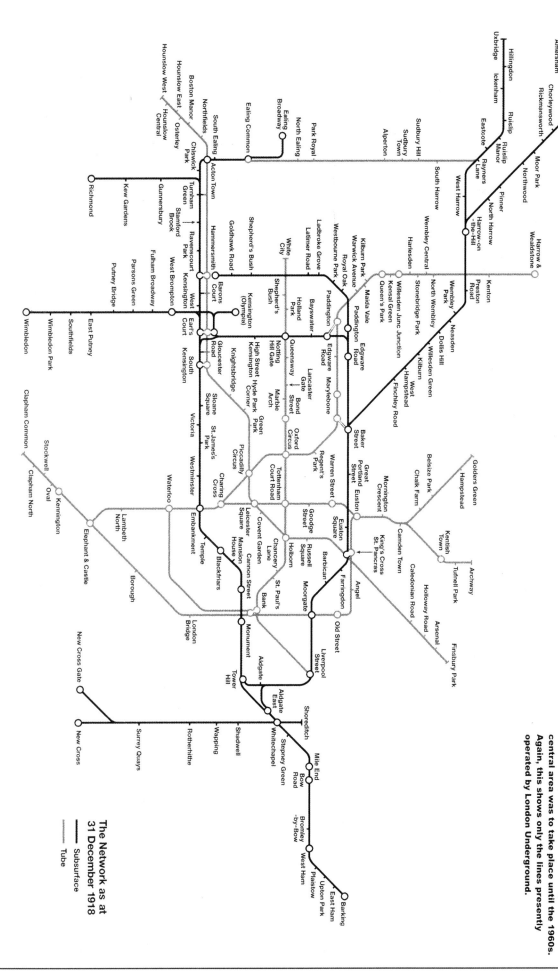

**The Network as at
31 December 1918**

— Subsurface
— Tube

**Growth of the system 2: This diagram shows
those parts of the present system which were
operational at the end of 1918. In 20 years,
the tube had become extremely well
established, and no further development in the
central area was to take place until the 1960s.
Again, this shows only the lines presently
operated by London Underground.**

3

FOR EVER
OUTWARDS?

By the beginning of the twentieth century, it was clear that the Metropolitan and its District counterpart needed to convert to electric traction. Logic dictated compatibility, and experiments were conducted between Earl's Court and High Street Kensington.

District victory

Perhaps predictably the companies failed to agree. Yerkes was firmly in favour of the dc system, and so it came to pass. The tremendous tasks of building the power stations at Lots Road and Neasden, many substations, and laying miles of cable, were at last put in hand.

Some 42 route km of the Metropolitan were electrified in three years and the length of the District to be electrified was even greater.

fundamentally from the District stock in that the latter opted for a single motor bogie and associated equipment, whereas the Metropolitan's motor cars had two motor bogies and thus no trailing bogie. Like the District, though, the Metropolitan quickly found BTH equipment to be much more reliable than that offered by Westinghouse.

From 1907, the Metropolitan took over the whole service provision on the Circle, and this hastened the conversion of some of the steam stock, built only a few years previously, to electric operation.

Left: *Early electric trains for the Metropolitan originally had lattice gates at the ends of each vehicle, attended by a gateman. This was soon deemed unsatisfactory where long journeys in the open air to places like Uxbridge were concerned. Later stock was built with end vestibules and earlier vehicles were converted. In the version with end doors as seen here, the lack of any centre door is noticeable, as is the small luggage compartment provided immediately behind the driver's cab.*
Author's collection

Two seven-car trains with open saloons and seating an average of 46 passengers a car were built. Larger and heavier than any tube stock, and with three 130kW motor cars in each train, they had a top speed of 97kph. These District cars bore unmistakable signs of their American origins. Henceforth carriages became cars, and bogies became trucks.

The District cars were mass-produced, with two-thirds of the 420 ordered constructed in France. Sliding doors were provided throughout, in the event to be hand-worked.

The last steam train operated on the Inner Circle on 22 September 1905. Not many months later, the major programme of electrification of both railways was completed using long, well-lit saloon cars. The District also purchased 10 electric locomotives.

There is little doubt that electrification did much for the railways and their passengers. Thus from Ealing Broadway to Mansion House, 40 steam trains taking 48 mins and charging a fare of 7d (2.9p) in 1901 were replaced by 187 electric trains taking 35 mins at a fare of 5d (2.1p) by 1913.

Metropolitan requirements

On the Metropolitan, steam traction would continue for both goods and express passenger work.

Deliveries of multiple-units were in batches from a variety of British manufacturers. These differed

A further 24 trains were built for the joint Metropolitan and GWR Hammersmith & City electrification, completed in 1906.

Metropolitan electric locos

The first 20 electric locomotives of 1904 were all were replaced by new machines built by Metropolitan Vickers at Barrow in 1922. These handled the increasingly heavy trains on the main-line out to Harrow and, when electrification was extended in 1925, to Rickmansworth.

These celebrated locomotives were equipped with 224kW motors, one geared to each of the four axles, with electro-magnetic control to provide special slow speed control for shunting purposes. Their overall length was 12.04m, and their weight 61.5 tonnes. Double-ended, they had dual Westinghouse compressed air and vacuum brakes, also trip cocks for train control (a separate one for each brake type). No. 15 was exhibited, with some rolling stock, at the Wembley Empire Exhibition in 1924/5, and carried a nameplate to that effect.

Long-term, two have survived. No. 12 *Sarah Siddons* is operational, while No 5 *John Hampden* is in the London Transport Museum.

The addition of the Uxbridge branch to the Metropolitan resulted in a quadrupling of the double track north of Finchley Road was undertaken as far as

Right: *The Metropolitan District's general extension of electrification was met with orders for the B stock, delivered from 1905 onwards. These were bulk orders, with the trains to general American design but built in both England and France. These cars had 30 years or so of life before they were retired under the 1935–40 New Works Programme.*
Ian Allan Library

Right: *This postcard view shows one of the first generation of Metropolitan electric locomotives, No. 10 from Westinghouse, with an Aylesbury train. It is seen near Willesden Green. Widening of this section to take four tracks was still to take place. On the near side is an express of the Great Central Railway. The middle vehicle of this seven-coach train is one of the Metropolitan's two celebrated Pullman cars, Mayflower and Galatea, which entered service on 1 June 1910. It is a sobering thought that consumption of alcohol on such a vehicle operating on the Underground nowadays would be an offence under the byelaws.*
Locomotive Publishing Co/ Author's collection

Wembley Park by 1915, and on the District the line was quadrupled west of Hammersmith in 1911. This work was later used for the westward extension of the Piccadilly. Both the surface railways needed new stock as a result. First Class passengers were provided for selectively until 1941.

The Birmingham RCW Co constructed two Pullman cars, Mayflower and Galatea, fitted out to Metropolitan specifications. These entered service in 1910 and were retained until 1939. Their main value was in the publicity they gave, rather than the revenue they generated.

The tube goes further

By the 1920s, the Underground map was beginning to look familiar to modern eyes, though as yet the extensive incursions into what became vast swathes of suburbs had hardly begun. The experience of Golders Green in Edwardian days had shown the potential, and this decade witnessed further extensions.

The Central London reached agreement with the Great Western that it would construct the Ealing & Shepherd's Bush Railway, and this opened in 1920. Electric power came from the GWR's Park Royal installation.

Legal powers to project the Hampstead tube from Golders Green to Edgware had been obtained as early as 1902, but it was not opened until 1923/4. A frequent Underground service was to galvanise Edgware's growth in a way that the modest offerings by the longer GNR route could never have done.

Integrating the C&SLR

Bolstered by cheap government money, the rehabilitation of the City & South London and its integration into the Hampstead tube began at last in 1922. Two distinct elements were involved: the enlargement of the old tunnels to standard bore, and the construction of the complex series of underground junctions at Camden Town. While work was in progress, further powers were obtained to extend south from Clapham to Morden, and to construct a new link from Embankment under the river to Waterloo and to junctions at Kennington. With the Edgware extension under way as well, the 'Edgware, Highgate & Morden Line', one of the names by which the combination was uneasily known, largely assumed its present Northern line form.

All the C&SLR's tunnels were bored out to the standard 3.56m diameter. There were some realignments to eliminate speed restrictions. Modernisation also covered the installation of standard Underground automatic signalling and the conversion of the power supply to fourth rail. Station platform tunnels were lengthened to 107 metres and the stations themselves were suitably updated, many being provided with escalators. Alone, City Road station between Euston and Angel did not reopen. The reconstruction effected a major improvement, and with new rolling stock as well, the running time between Euston and Clapham Common was reduced by one quarter.

To Morden, only

The Southern Railway drew a physical as well as a metaphorical line across the tube's path with the building of the Wimbledon & Sutton Railway. Morden thus became the terminus. As so often in south London, tube construction was problematic owing to waterlogged ground, especially at Tooting Broadway. From a final 'cut-and-cover' section, the tube emerged into open-air cutting at Morden, where a three-track/five-platform face layout was built. The tracks continued beyond to extensive stabling facilities on the surface. A conscious effort was made to make all the stations on the extension conspicuous, and the angular surface buildings made much use of Portland stone.

Morden station forecourt became a busy and important bus-rail interchange point for onward travel.

Work then began south of Charing Cross with a new line to Embankment (present names), Waterloo and Kennington. Here, the new connection gave cross-platform interchange for passengers towards Morden. A terminal loop was provided for reversing direction. The opening of the Kennington extension coincided with the completion to Morden, and on 13 September 1926 work was finished for the time being.

Left: *Of the twenty locomotives built by Metropolitan Vickers in Barrow, No. 12* Sarah Siddons *survives in working order for use on rail tours as required. In sunshine after rain, she shows off her new paint at the depot at Acton on 9 March 2008. This is the second set of premises of the London Transport Museum, where some larger exhibits and the reserve stock are kept.* John Glover

LIVE IN METRO-LAND

Metroland

Jointly with the Great Central Railway, the Metropolitan built a 3km branch from Moor Park to Croxley Green and Watford, or, rather, to the edge of Cassiobury Park, through which the railway was not allowed to pass. This unsatisfactory terminal arrangement severely limited the practical usefulness of the line, which has always remained something of a backwater. Services commenced in 1925.

The housing boom of the inter-war years transformed great expanses of open country around London into street upon street of detached and semi-detached houses. Perhaps the most sustained attempt to stimulate suburban living was the building of Metro-Land.

During the interwar period, 4,000 homes were built in Middlesex and Buckinghamshire on the back of the Metropolitan Railway Co., with the concurrent expansion of the railway facilities. That this was possible was in large measure owing to the Metropolitan's ability to exploit its excessive land holdings in the area to the benefit of the railway's finances. British railway companies were generally discouraged or forbidden from ownership of land which they did not require for carrying on their main business.

Continued congestion on the Metropolitan mainline resulted in the four-tracking reaching out to Harrow by 1932, the same year in which the 7.24km Stanmore branch was completed. Both schemes were financed by cheap government money, provided for the relief of unemployment.

Upminster

The extension of electrification to Upminster was to serve the vast new London County Council Becontree housing estate. Two additional lines were laid in for the new service to the north of the Tilbury tracks by the London Midland & Scottish Railway as successors to the LT&S company, with three more stations opened.

Piccadilly goes north

The Great Northern, Piccadilly & Brompton Railway, to give the line its earlier title, had provided a direct connection from its northern terminus at Finsbury Park to the West End from 1906. Finsbury Park was one massive railway interchange, to which was added the traffic from the trams and motor buses. The tube terminus was built on Great Northern property, and one of the consequences had been an undertaking given in 1902 that the Piccadilly would not be extended northwards without GNR consent.

By 1925, with 30,000 passengers changing between different forms of transport daily, the public pressure to relieve the congestion was intense.

Part of the problem was finance. One result was the Act of 1927 under which the Underground Group was able to borrow capital at 3% to finance the Piccadilly improvements. These were started in 1930, following the waiving (under protest) of the London & North Eastern Railway veto five years earlier.

This line to Cockfosters runs partly in tube, and partly across undulating country. For the 6.5km from Finsbury Park until it emerges at Arnos Grove, the line runs in twin tunnels. From here, the line shortly enters an 850m tunnel, towards the far end of which is Southgate station. Cutting followed by viaduct and embankment takes the line to Oakwood and Cockfosters terminus, between which points are the highest and coldest car sheds on the Underground system, 84m above sea level.

Further expansion

Housing in places like Hounslow, Ealing and Harrow led to a decision to balance the working of the Piccadilly line by extending it at the other end. Services were projected concurrently to the west and northwest, largely by the adaptation of existing lines. By 1933, the Piccadilly had been extended in stages from Hammersmith to Hounslow West and to Uxbridge.

In the central-London section, Leicester Square, Green Park, Hyde Park Corner and Knightsbridge were extensively rebuilt. The classic rebuilding was that of Piccadilly Circus (1928). The solution was to create a 1,400m ticket hall area 4.5m below the surface of the Circus itself, surrounded by a circular walkway which was accessed from five subways leading to the street and directly into the basement of a prestigious department store.

Three of the lesser-used stations were closed, with the deliberate intention of speeding up the services.

The 1933 rebuilding at Holborn was to make it an interchange between the Central line and the Piccadilly, which previously had separate stations.

Left: The station at Hendon Central was opened in 1923 and before long was built on with the results as seen here. This photograph was taken from the other side of a very busy road junction on the A41 on 7 May 2008, but shows the Palladian-style columns supporting the portico. Hendon Central consists of a single island platform in the open reached by stairs down. Northbound trains enter the 1km single-bore Burroughs Tunnels immediately after leaving the station. John Glover

Left: With the difference that the station platforms at Brent Cross are on an embankment, the buildings at street level are very similar to Hendon Central. Here, though, development passed by, and they remain unencumbered. There is a modest car park outside, though this seems to be used as much for those visiting the convenience store to the left as for Underground passengers. The station was renamed (from Brent) in 1976; the shopping centre is a short walk away. It is 1 June 2009. John Glover

FOR EVER OUTWARDS?

A new approach

Fears of monopoly power in the nineteenth century receded in the twentieth. 1915 saw the London Electric Railways Facilities Act, which allowed the C&SLR, CLR, LER, MDR and also the LGOC to create a pooled revenue agreement into which all moneys collected would be paid, and each would draw upon in agreed proportions. The first steps by government to co-ordinate London's transport were taken by the setting up of the Ministry of Transport in 1919, and the benefits of mass production and the planned approach became part of the general ethos.

By 1931, it was possible for Herbert Morrison to say when introducing the second reading of the London Passenger Transport Bill into the House that 'Competition must go; it stultifies progress, endangers the standard of life of the workpeople in the industry, and is too expensive'. The Bill, first promoted by a Labour administration, was subsequently enacted by the new National government. The LPTB was to be self-supporting and unsubsidised, with a degree of public control but non-political management.

Before the Board

The achievements of the Underground and the Metropolitan should perhaps be recorded. In 1932, the last full year of their separate existence, the trains of what was to become London Transport in popular parlance carried 498 million passengers using 2,951 passenger vehicles. Fig. 3.1 shows how passenger journeys were spread almost equally between the surface and the tube lines.

Figure 3.1: The Underground in 1932

Company	Locomotives	Passenger Vehicles	Passengers (m)
Subsurface lines			
Metropolitan	57	00719	119.7
District	07	00564	126.5
Total	**64**	**1,283**	**246.2**
Tube lines			
London Electric	-	1,295	149.8
City & South London	-	0,114	061.2
Central London	-	0,259	041.2
Total	**-**	**1,668**	**252.2**
Total to LPTB	**64**	**2,951**	**498.4**

Note: The Metropolitan totals include the GN&C; of the company's 57 locomotives, 36 were steam. The vehicle stock also included 18 parcels and 544 goods vehicles.

The Beck diagram

January 1933 was to see the first printing of Harry Beck's diagrammatic representation of London Underground, at first as a pocket folder and later as a poster. With this stylised representation, all attempts at geographical accuracy as used in the maps up to that time, ceased. The only other physical feature is a stylised representation of the Thames.

Beck's original depicted an Underground rather smaller than it is today. It was immediately successful, and has remained so ever since. A complete redrawing was undertaken by Harold Hutchison in 1960, and again by Paul Garbutt in 1964. Most of the line colours are long established, though subtle changes have taken place over the years, certainly in terms of the exact shade of the colours used.

Garbutt's work remains the basis of the computerised version seen today. Sadly, though, it is now called 'Tube map' by London Underground. As readers will be aware, it covers much more than just the tubes, and a map it is not. However, a clumsy attempt in 2009 to remove the Thames from the pocket folder version was swiftly rebuffed by the Mayor, Boris Johnson, who felt that this, the only geographical feature, should be retained.

The Johnston typeface

While the Underground map is a well-known feature of every station platform, the same can be said for poster advertising which brings in useful revenue.

However, posters also compete for attention with the really necessary information for the passenger. To distinguish the station nameboards and make them stand out, the bull's eye symbol was devised in 1908.

Left: *This striking tower serves to mark the presence of Osterley station alongside the Great West Road (A4). Motorists may or may not feel that the Piccadilly line can offer them anything they want, but they can hardly fail to be aware of its existence. The station was opened as a new station in 1934 (replacing Osterley & Spring Grove) and is seen here 69 years later in 2003.* John Glover

Left: *The platform lighting was only one of the many facets of the station to which attention was given in the 1930s. Although the fittings have now been replaced, that at Eastcote demonstrates this well in March 2003.* John Glover

The lettering styles then available were seen as seriously deficient, and the upshot was the commissioning of a new typeface. This was to be simple, clear and open, and also modern. It was to be used exclusively to present information from the company, as distinct from advertisers.

The result was a revolution in the appearance of the Underground. The Group's then Traffic Manager, Frank Pick, was largely responsible. He commissioned Edward Johnston to design both the bullseye and the lettering form which still bears his name. The Johnston typeface was first used in 1916. It is one of the earliest examples of a modern sans-serif. In 1979, LT would commission the New Johnston family of typefaces, to take full advantage of developing technology.

Ownership of the Johnston typeface is now vested in Transport for London, and is fully protected by copyright law. Today, New Johnston is intended to give the organisation a distinctive and uniform image, very much as it has always done.

Right: *The roundel is seen here on 23 July 2009 in one of its more ornate forms, outside Arnos Grove station. The marketing value of this symbol has been exploited now for a century, albeit with continuous and usually subtle changes over time. It is recognised the world over for what it is, though how many would mention Transport for London when asked is another matter.*
John Glover

Left: *Rayners Lane was another of the reconstructions by Charles Holden. This is the main station building. Originally, entrance to the station could also be made from the opposite side, but this was blocked as part of the installation of the Underground Ticketing System. 28 June 2008. John Glover*

Left: *Cockfosters, constructed in 1932, has a central track with a platform both sides, and two more on the outsides of the islands. The roof allows much natural light to reach the enclosed area, as seen here on 10 April 2008. The extra post-Moorgate measures to prevent trains ramming the concourse have meant that the buffer stops have now been located a good bit further away from the ticket gates than intended by the designers, but judicious planting has improved that area considerably. John Glover*

Right: *The LPTB was quick to rid itself of all operations north of Aylesbury, and this included the Brill branch in 1935. This is the classic view of Metropolitan No. 41 at Wood Siding with the one coach. This was by all accounts more than sufficient for the branch passenger traffic offering. That the Underground should encompass such oddities is perhaps surprising, but the not dissimilar saga of the Ongar branch was then still many years in the future.* Author's collection

London Passenger Transport Board

The new Board, which quickly became known as London Transport, was dominated by Lord Ashfield as Chairman and Frank Pick as Vice Chairman and Chief Executive.

The purpose of the Board was set out in an initial LPTB Press Announcement: 'The Board is a public authority appointed under Act of Parliament charged with responsibility for providing an adequate and properly co-ordinated system of public transport within the London Passenger Transport Area. It is required to take such steps as it considers necessary for avoiding wasteful, competitive services and for extending and improving London's passenger transport facilities, so as to meet the growing needs of the vast population working and dwelling within the area over which the Board's operations extend'.

That area was defined as being roundly within 48km (30 miles) of Charing Cross, with a population at that time of around 9.5 million. The suggestion that competition was inherently wasteful is an interesting comment on how times have since changed.

The Board had a duty to break even, and to fix their fares and charges accordingly. They were also given borrowing powers for capital purposes. The vesting date was 1 July 1933.

Revenue pooling

The only omissions from the 1933 Act were the 'Big Four' main-line railway companies. A pooling scheme was established which covered suburban traffic in an area considerably larger than that of the present Greater London. The passenger receipts of the LPTB and those of main-line railways on journeys wholly within the London Passenger Transport Area were pooled, and after deducting the operating expenses, revenue was divided in the ratio of approximately 63% to the Board, and 37% to the main-line railways as a whole. The aim was to limit competition and to make more possible electrification and other betterment schemes of the main-line railways.

Metropolitan closures

The closure of the Brill branch with fewer than 50 passengers and 20 tons of freight a day took place in late 1935. The Aylesbury–Verney Junction service followed the Brill branch into oblivion the following summer.

Bakerloo to Stanmore

A major shortcoming of the Metropolitan main line was the capacity limitation represented by the two-track section between Baker Street and Finchley Road.

The LPTB decided to construct a new tube line from Baker Street to Finchley Road with two intermediate stations. This would enable the Bakerloo trains to run to Wembley Park and then over the Metropolitan's branch to Stanmore. The Bakerloo trains were given exclusive use of the two lines in the middle of the four track formation.

As part of the plan, the Metropolitan services would run non-stop over the 3.4km between Baker Street and Finchley Road and again for the 7.2km thence to Wembley Park. Today, what is now the Jubilee Line takes 19 mins between Baker Street and Wembley Park; with one stop only the Met takes 12 mins.

At Neasden, new depot facilities were built for both lines.

As part of the same development programme, the rest of the Bakerloo station platforms were lengthened to 115m to take seven cars instead of six. Resignalling enabled extra trains to be run.

Other major station works under the Board in this period included the resiting of Aldgate East to free up the triangular junction, while Uxbridge station was rebuilt on a new site closer to the town centre. Both were completed in 1938. King's Cross Metropolitan station was also updated, with works completed in 1941.

New Works Programme

Before work started on these improvements though, the London Passenger Transport Board launched one of its major acts of policy — the New Works Programme, 1935–40. Originally estimated to involve an expenditure of £40 million, and planned for completion by about 1940, this was by far the biggest single programme of transport development ever undertaken in the London area.

A major feature was the projection of tube lines up to the surface and extended over newly electrified main-line tracks. Only a fragment of the works was completed before World War 2, but two fundamental principles were established. These were:

Suburban lines carrying a dense traffic within the London Transport Area should be electrified as soon as circumstances permitted, and as far as practicable, the Underground should work short-distance suburban services, and link them with their own tubes or surface lines.

The main proposals as they directly affected the Underground were as follows:

Central Line. Extension from Liverpool Street to Stratford and over the LNER tracks to Loughton, also thence to Ongar. New tube constructed from Leytonstone to Newbury Park, then by LNER route via Hainault and Woodford. Extension west from North Acton Junction to West Ruislip (later to Denham) over additional tracks laid alongside GWR Birmingham main-line. Withdrawal of LNER/GWR services.

Northern Line. Highly complex extensions from Moorgate–Finsbury Park line over the LNER to both the Alexandra Palace branch (diverging at Highgate) and to East Finchley, meeting at the latter with a new projection of the Archway line. Trains would continue over the LNER to Finchley Central, junction for the High Barnet branch. Trains would also continue over the LNER's branch to Edgware via Mill Hill East. There would be a new extension from an enlarged Edgware Underground station to Bushey Heath.

Metropolitan Line. Quadrupling of the section Harrow-on-the-Hill–Rickmansworth and extension of electrification from Rickmansworth to Amersham, including the Chesham branch.

No extensions of the Central Line were ready for traffic before the war, but platform extensions to 130m to take eight-car trains in the central core and conversion of the original third-rail electrification to the fourth-rail London Transport standard were completed in 1938.

The Northern Line extension north of Archway was completed to High Barnet, with electric services starting in April 1940 and reaching Mill Hill East in 1941.

Only minor preparatory work for the Metropolitan electrification was undertaken.

War begins

The outbreak of the war saw the control of the undertaking passing to the Minister of Transport on 1 September 1939. This was exercised through the Railway Executive Committee, which acted as an agent for the Minister. In 1939 the Board employed 17,812 staff on their railways.

Left: *Geographical expansion of what is essentially a Metro system cannot continue forever, especially to such modest habitations as Verney Junction. This is how the erstwhile terminus of the Metropolitan looked in 1994; the track is that of the now mothballed Bicester to Bletchley line. 'Met' trains once used the bay at the other side of the platform shown, their route curving away immediately to the right and reaching Baker Street 80km later. This service ceased in 1936.* John Glover

Above: *The Metropolitan steam locomotives were sold by the London Passenger Transport Board after they took control in 1933, with the remaining revenue-earning work of hauling the Metropolitan passenger trains north of Rickmansworth and the goods traffic subcontracted to the LNER. This company took the locomotives too in 1937; this is K class 2-6-4T as LNER L2 class No. 6160. It bears the NE inscription, which was all that was provided in wartime.* Author's collection

Right: *Some station upgrades in the later 1930s included the incorporation of tiles of relevant local interest. These were the work of Harold Stabler. The subject of this one is clearly St Paul's, and that is at least one of the stations at which these decorative tiles can be found.* John Glover

Arising from this, the government effectively guaranteed company net revenues. The Board's traffic, swollen at times by troop movements, was substantially reduced by the evacuation, by the blackout, and later by the bombing of London. The population in the area served fell by 2,700,000 so that by late 1944 only 7,147,000 remained. The financial implications were not welcome.

The replacement of rolling stock came to an end, and a reduction in maintenance programmes, brought about by an acute shortage of labour and materials, had to be accepted. At the same time, with many staff away in the Forces, there was a need to make a contribution to the national effort in aircraft manufacture and war supplies generally. Rolling stock and equipment were thus maintained in service with great difficulty.

Wartime precautions

The war formed a test of altogether unprecedented severity. The first concern was to take adequate air raid precautions. The most obvious threat to the Underground in central London was that of flooding. To counter that, a complete system of electrically-operated floodgates was installed on those lines each side of the Thames so that the underwater sections could be isolated. These construction works represented the most major disruption of the system during the entire war period.

Other less extensive preparatory work included: the duplication and paralleling of electricity supply cables, modifying ventilation arrangements to minimise the effects of a poison gas attack, strengthening the structures of essential buildings ranging from generating stations to traffic control offices, and use of disused tube stations as secure accommodation for government and other purposes.

The Aldwych branch was closed for the duration and used to store items from the British Museum.

The blackout regulations produced major difficulties. As well as all the stations, depots and workshops, every vehicle had to be fitted with special lighting which was the minimum possible to enable the job to be done. Miles of netting covered all but the centre of the windows on underground cars.

Signals had to be hooded and dimmed, whilst all kinds of maintenance work became that much more awkward. The strain on passengers and staff alike was great.

A classless society

The tube lines of what became London Underground have always offered one class travel, but not so the subsurface lines. First Class facilities were withdrawn gradually, but on 11 September 1941 the Minister of War Transport announced that from 6 October all trains which both began and ended their journeys within the London Passenger Transport Area would be Third Class only. The aim was to get the best possible use of all the cars available.

Bombing

Most bombing incidents from August 1940 onwards resulted in partial line closures for periods of 10 days or less. Those that took longer to repair included Balham (14 October 1940), Bank (11 January 1941), and between King's Cross and Euston Square (10 May 1941). The worst incident took place at the then unopened station at Bethnal Green (3 March 1943).

Over 2,000 incidents relating to damage to railway buildings were recorded, and 1,050 cases of damage to rolling stock. Nineteen railway cars were totally destroyed.

What were passengers supposed to do? Displayed notices, headed 'If you are in a train during an air raid or when an alert is sounded', gave advice. The instructions were 'Do not leave the train between stations unless so requested by a railway official. Should a gas attack be suspected, close all windows and ventilators, refrain from smoking, and do not touch any outside part of a car. Always have your gas mask with you.'

Tube station shelters

The tube stations made natural shelters from the bombing. The first official use was on 7 September 1940. Sanitary arrangements were hastily installed, with a drainage system at 81 stations eventually allowing sewage to be pumped to the surface. A refreshment service provided by train or otherwise was feeding 120,000 nightly in late 1940. Most slept on the platforms, although bunks for 22,800 were built. Later, bunk allocations were provided by ticket, and medical posts, washing facilities, storage for bedding and even small libraries eventually made an appearance.

The peak night was 27 September 1940, when 177,000 spent the night as guests of the London Underground. Thereafter, numbers declined gradually.

At the request of the Ministry of Food the LPTB added a public catering department to their range of activities, to supply food to shelterers every night. Catering stores were set up at Wood Lane in the former CLR workshops, and supplies included items such as electric boilers, as well as the food which was distributed in containers.

Eight new deep-level shelters were constructed below some existing Northern (and Central) Line platforms, in the hope that in peacetime they could be utilised as part of an express tube network.

Below: These were wartime conditions at South Tottenham on 1 March 1940. This was described as 'new' rolling stock for the LNER/LPTB electrification scheme being hauled from the carriage works by a steam locomotive. The train is taking the line towards Coppermill Junction and, presumably, Stratford. Postponement of electrification works for the duration had all sorts of complex results in terms of the construction, usage and storage of rolling stock.
Ian Allan Library

The section of uncompleted tunnel between Leytonstone and Gants Hill was turned into an aircraft component factory. It was installed by the Plessey Company in 1942, converting the 4km stretch into a wartime production line employing more than 2,000 workers.

Underground traffic

The volume of traffic carried reflected the course of the war. Depressed traffic levels in 1940 and 1941 slowly recovered with the intensification of the war effort and greater movement of HM Forces. Services were also restricted due to coal shortages limiting electricity generation. Although initially the number of passengers carried fell faster than the drop in car km operated, the later expansion of demand was met by further restrictions on the service provided.

By 1945, 543 million passenger journeys were catered for by 261 million car km, which meant that trains were getting a lot more crowded. Here was the genesis of a problem which was to dog the

Underground for the next 20 years. What happens when system capacity consistently fails to meet the demands placed upon it?

The post-war world

In the words of the 1945 Annual Report, 'Shortages of staff and fuel remained and no immediate increases in services were possible.' Rather, victory brought some embarrassment to the Board, for the general reaction after six years of war manifested itself in a desire for enjoyment and celebration, and heavier loadings were the result. The focus of all the effort had gone, the staff were exhausted, and the system was run-down and lacking new equipment.

The longer-term scene was influenced by the planners. In 1943, Sir Patrick Abercrombie finished his huge survey of the planning needs of London; it was full of visions of an orderly, beautiful city to take over after the war. One result was a plan to build new underground railways all over the central area, co-ordinating the efforts of the main-line railways and the Underground. Another was to confirm the creation of a 'Green Belt' to surround the capital and limit urban sprawl, which was now seen to be growing at an alarming rate and something to be discouraged. The catch was the complete lack of public money to make any advance towards the goals; not to put too fine a point on it, there wasn't any left.

Writing their own epitaph in the 1947 Annual Report, the Board recorded that they had 'sought to provide a passenger transport service, by rail and road, worthy of London as a great metropolitan city; at the same time, they have pursued a long-term policy of financial soundness, supported by an appropriate fares structure which could also be justified both by the adequacy of the services and the efficiency of their operation'. Looking forward, they added, perhaps a little plaintively, that they 'had done all in their power to press on with new railway works and to obtain new supplies of rolling stock.' The emerging post-war situation was not encouraging for capital intensive schemes.

FINSBURY PARK
COCKFOSTERS

PICCADILLY CIRCUS
LEICESTER SQUARE
COVENT GARDEN
HOLBORN (KINGSWAY)
RUSSELL SQUARE
KINGS CROSS, ST. PANCRAS
CALEDONIAN ROAD
HOLLOWAY ROAD
ARSENAL (HIGHBURY HILL)
FINSBURY PARK
MANOR HOUSE
TURNPIKE LANE
WOOD GREEN
BOUNDS GREEN
ARNOS GROVE
SOUTHGATE
OAKWOOD
COCKFOSTERS

GREEN PARK

GREEN PARK

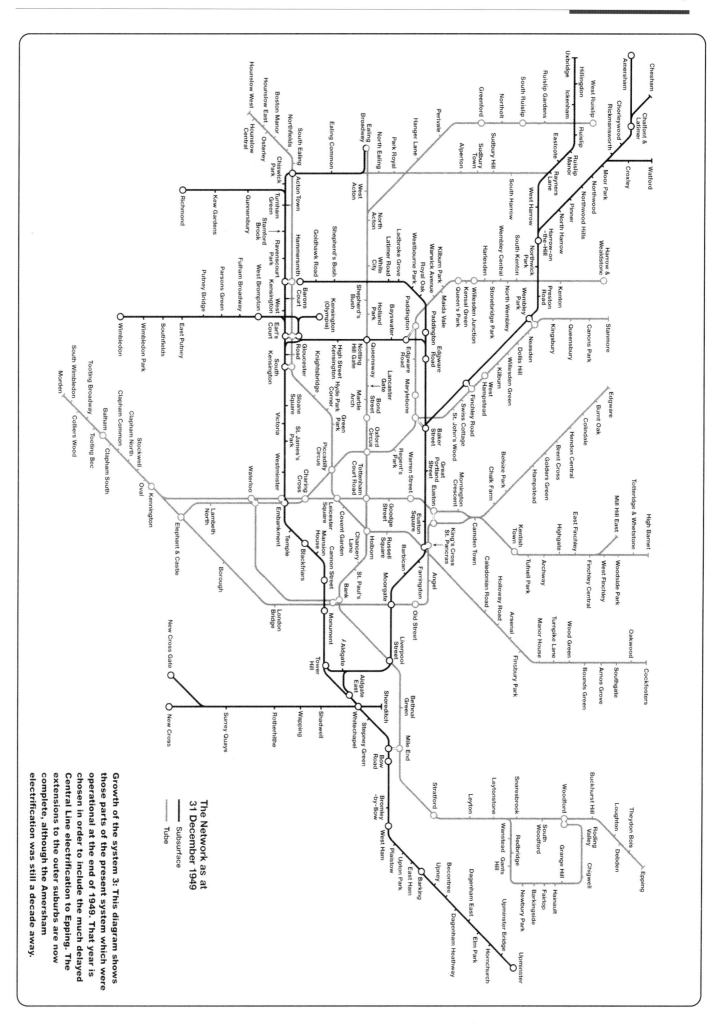

The Network as at 31 December 1949

Subsurface

Tube

Growth of the system 3: This diagram shows those parts of the present system which were operational at the end of 1949. That year is chosen in order to include the much delayed Central Line electrification to Epping. The extensions to the outer suburbs are now complete, although the Amersham electrification was still a decade away.

4

THE DOLDRUM YEARS

The Transport Act, 1947 saw London
Transport nationalised for, as it turned out,
the first time. The new body was the
London Transport Executive (LTE), under
the direction and control of the British
Transport Commission (BTC). Vesting
took place on 1 January 1948.

The new organisation

The Executive had the obligation, in conjunction with the Railway Executive, of providing an efficient, adequate, economical and properly integrated system of passenger transport, by rail and by road, in the London Transport Area.

Fares became the province of the newly-created Transport Tribunal, to which the BTC had to make application for variations.

In practice, the LTE was left mainly to its own devices. There was a minor rash of boundary changes. Notably, LT was put in charge of the section from Harrow-on-the-Hill to south of Aylesbury, the Chesham and the Watford branches, and it also acquired the East London line and the District east of Whitechapel.

Central Line goes west

The New Works programme had promised great things for Central Line users and a new above-ground White City station was opened in 1947. The twin island platforms retained the right-hand running inherited from the old layout, giving a curious back-to-front feeling to the station. Further west, a flyover was built to resume normal left-hand running. At North Acton, a new burrowing junction enabled West Ruislip trains to diverge from the Ealing line without crossing its metals.

The West Ruislip trains paralleled the (now) former Birmingham main line, and much of the Underground was carried on a succession of bridges and viaducts.

On the south side of the line at Ruislip Gardens is the Underground's extensive Ruislip Depot. This major facility can be accessed both from the Central and the Metropolitan's Uxbridge branch.

From West Ruislip to Epping is nearly 55km, the longest continuous journey which can be undertaken on the Underground.

Management and ownership of the infrastructure both here and in the east were transferred from British Railways to London Transport in stages, a process completed in 1963.

Continuing east

Eastwards from Liverpool Street, the Central Line was extended in new tunnels to Mile End where there is cross-platform interchange with the District, then to Stratford. Here, it rises to the surface and offers cross-platform interchange to the main-line Shenfield services.

From here the Central dived back into tube tunnel, joining the former LNER metals west of Leyton station. At Leytonstone the route forked, some trains continuing to Woodford, while others entered the new tube, no longer serving as a wartime factory, to surface again at Newbury Park.

Here the tube joined the LNER tracks from Ilford (later abandoned), and trains proceeded to Hainault with its extensive depot facilities. Services continued to Woodford, by which time trains are facing back towards central London.

The main-line services continued to Loughton, and later to Epping as the new terminus for electric trains. This was reached on 25 September 1949.

Left: Of the former Great Eastern stations on the Central Line eastern extensions, Loughton was the only one to have been completely rebuilt. Two island platforms serve three tracks between them, the central track being used for terminating trains and thus having platforms on both sides. A westbound train of 1992 stock approaches on 26 May 2001. The design of the platform seating is an Underground classic. John Glover

Right: *This train is of 1926 tube stock, nominally known as standard, but in practice the various builds over a considerable period made it anything but! Pre-1938 stock is a rather safer description. This is a Central Line working to West Ruislip, with car No. 3628 leading and probably not long before these trains were replaced by the 1962 'silver' stock.* Electrail Collection (4401)

Right: *What do you do with a remote and all but disconnected piece of the British Railways system which retains steam traction but whose traffic levels are exceedingly light? The wisdom of the day led to electrification and use of tube stock in 1957; this undated view is of a less than pristine BR Class 'F5' 2-4-2T locomotive no. 67218 arriving at Epping from Ongar before electric services commenced.* Author's collection

The wholly rural single-track 9.85km branch from Epping to Ongar was run by British Railways with steam services, until it too was electrified in 1957. This marked the completion of the Central Line work, more or less as planned.

Northern Heights

This project was left at the state which it had reached in 1941, when the Northern Line reached Mill Hill East. British Railways withdrew their Alexandra Palace passenger service in 1954, but continued freight traffic on all branches until that too ceased in the late 1960s. The abandoned works included the Underground's 4.61km extension from Edgware to Bushey Heath, since Green Belt policies had determined that the proposed housing growth would not now take place.

What next?

The costs and benefits of passenger transport are distributed on a much wider canvas than the company and its customers. It was not merely a private matter between two parties to a commercial transaction, especially in an age which believed in the efficacy of the planned approach.

From the earliest days, entrepreneurs realised that whilst transport facilities might be provided profitably to meet a demand which was already there, the provision of such facilities in themselves could stimulate traffic and increase the values of the surrounding properties. The problem has always been that while the railway interests would benefit from the generated traffic revenues, this was not enough to finance extensions and regeneration of the systems. The gains to property values accrue to their owners.

Thus the extensions of the Underground under the New Works Programme 1935-40 became possible only because of the availability of cheap government loan capital.

Cheap finance, or grants, tended to set the scene; if it was investment in urban railways that was wanted, funding of capital costs would have to be mainly a matter for either central or local government.

Both public and political interest in passenger transport in the post-war years was low. They were indeed the doldrums years, characterised by little activity or progress.

Victoria Line

Of the British Transport Commission's 1949 Working Party proposals 'Route C' was the only new scheme to be pursued to completion. This was to be a new tube from the Tottenham and Edmonton area via Finsbury Park, King's Cross, Euston, Oxford Circus, Green Park, Victoria, Vauxhall, Stockwell, Brixton, Streatham to East Croydon. Branch lines on the alignment of the Cambridge Road and from Seven Sisters to Walthamstow were 'possibly desirable'.

There, in all essence, was the Victoria Line, which opened 20 years later between 1968 and 1972.

Why did it take so long? The major problem turned out to be in persuading government that it was indeed in their best interest to fund its construction. Attitudes tended to the hostile, with capital scarce to the point of near invisibility. If a commercial rate of return was being sought, then there were other more attractive investments. In vain was it argued that it was London (rather than London Transport) which stood to gain.

The long-drawn-out struggle to achieve authorisation eventually turned to the newly developed science of social cost-benefit analysis. Through this it was demonstrated rather than asserted that most of the benefits fell elsewhere, and that road users rather than rail passengers would be the principal beneficiaries.

Therefore, the argument went, the gains to the wider community were a sufficient and acceptable justification for building the line, even though it would be a disaster for London Transport should they have to fulfil a commercial rate of return.

Authorisation

The government finally approved the construction of the 16km Victoria Line from Victoria to Walthamstow on 20 August 1962. General principles were:
- avoidance of curves sharper than 400m radius
- stations to be built on a hump profile, giving a falling gradient to accelerate a train leaving a station and a rising gradient approaching it
- tunnel diameter sufficient to minimise air resistance, and
- line to be as straight as possible between any two points, not following street patterns above.

These ideals had to be modified as necessary to fit the line into the pattern of existing infrastructure, but work could now begin in earnest.

A number of other important schemes were carried out in this period.

Left: *Abandoned works on the Northern Heights electrification included what would have been Highgate High Level station, with stairs down to the below-ground ticket office which would serve both this and the present deep-level Highgate. The partly modernised, partly GNR station was to be a single island platform situated between two tunnels. The track has long since been lifted and the site is now completely overgrown.* Author's collection

THE DOLDRUM YEARS

District

With the electrification of the London, Tilbury & Southend lines pending, a major upgrade was needed to remove the delays caused by junction working. Thus a complex series of flyovers and diveunders was constructed west of Barking, with crossovers removed elsewhere.

At Upminster, a new Underground depot was constructed in 1959 with a 34-train capacity. Points were power-operated and controlled from the tower, with instructions being given to drivers via trackside loudspeakers. Fortunately, there were few houses nearby.

The track layout in the Earl's Court/High Street Kensington/South Kensington triangle was sadly deficient in terms of junction conflicts. Works in 1957 involved reversing the running direction on two tracks and changing the crossing positions. Further simplification took place in 1969, and this resulted in one wide island platform at South Kensington serving both directions.

In 1959, a practically new station was brought into use at Notting Hill Gate, serving both the Central and the District/Circle Lines. Platform extension work was undertaken at both Blackfriars and Westminster.

Right: *The electrification of the LNER line from Finsbury Park to East Finchley and Alexandra Palace for the Underground was progressing nicely. A new substation had been built, some of the cabling was in place, and a substantial reconstruction of Crouch End station was under way. This is seen here from the Finsbury Park end on 10 April 2005. The half-constructed buildings on the overbridge bear witness to the work carried out, and the platforms were brought up to standard. Today, this is no more than an interesting feature on a pleasant recreational pathway. The last BR trains called here in 1954.* John Glover

Right: *At platform level on the subsurface station at South Kensington, the multiple tracks once provided were whittled down to two during the 1950s, requiring only what is now a decidedly wide island platform. Looking east on 22 April 2009, a D stock train disappears towards central London, regaining a conventional two-track formation, while on the left can be seen the space in which a second eastbound track once stood. The 'cut' for this part of the District was not subsequently covered, though this scene demonstrates that it was not a particularly complicated task.* John Glover

Amersham electrification

The last of the 1935–40 projects was the Metropolitan main line rebuilding. Whereas the pre-war scheme had envisaged the conversion of 'steam' stock to electric multiple unit use, galloping dilapidation coupled with the growing demand which was apparent by the mid-1950s secured authorisation using new stock in 1956. Work was thus started on the four-tracking (to Watford South Junction) and electrification of the Metropolitan line north of Harrow. The scheme was allowed to proceed, as it extended way beyond the Green Belt to areas where development was to be encouraged.

Physical site work started in 1958, and the changeover to total multiple unit working using the new 'A' stock was took place on 11 September 1961. The widening scheme was not completed until 1962.

Resignalling was carried out as part of the project, and this provided for standard BR four-aspect signalling on the fast lines (where speeds of up to 112km/h were permitted) and through to Amersham, owing to the dual use with BR trains to and from Marylebone. Standard LT two-aspects sufficed elsewhere. Following completion, London Transport surrendered all interests beyond Amersham or, to be precise, at Mantles Wood, north of a point close to Network Rail milepost 25¼ (40.63km, but 87.08km in LU speak), and designated by a boundary marker.

Transport Act 1962

The BTC was abolished under the Transport Act 1962 and the Executive reconstituted as the London Transport Board. As such, it was responsible directly to the Minister. The separation from British Railways was all but complete and each would henceforth go its own way.

It was the financial duty of each of the new Boards thus created to ensure that revenue was sufficient to meet the costs incurred which were chargeable to revenue, taking one year with another.

The powers of the Transport Tribunal were restricted by introducing a requirement for charges to be reasonable. (This was subtly different from the bus industry, where the Traffic Commissioners were to ensure that fares were not unreasonable).

Fares were thus left largely to the Board's discretion, with a rider that the Tribunal should do nothing to prevent them from levying the charges needed to discharge their financial duty.

Vesting date was 1 January 1963.

Barbican diversion

The 1960s were the age of the big holes in London, when the scars left from the bombing of World War 2 were finally healed. The Barbican was one of the largest construction projects, and at the behest of the City of

Above: The first trial run of an electric train to Chesham on the Metropolitan took place on 15 August 1960. This was made up of T stock, as the first deliveries of the A stock which has monopolised all services on the outer stretches of the Metropolitan ever since were still 18 months away. Here a short formation stands in the main platform (there was at this time also a bay), with the signalbox behind. The date is 8 September 1960. Although colour lights were to replace the semaphores operated from this box, this was after electric traction had arrived. The box itself still stands.
G. W. Sharpe Collection
SD103

London, London Transport diverted the Metropolitan to a straighter and more southerly route between Aldersgate (now Barbican) and Moorgate.

This work first entailed the moving of the Widened Lines. The 450 metres of new railway were constructed by the 'cut-and-cover' method, reinforced concrete being used both to enclose the line and support the Barbican development above. This work was completed in 1965.

Victoria Line

Meanwhile, progress with Victoria Line construction by September 1966 saw the work of the shields cutting the running and station tunnels complete. The whole of the line is underground apart from the depot, located at Northumberland Park and reached from Seven Sisters.

Two of the major works deserve special mention. At Oxford Circus, the Victoria Line tubes swing out to flank the Bakerloo on both sides, thus providing the ideal cross-platform interchange. Building this composite station below ground took longer than any other along the line, and the only visible surface evidence of the day and night activity going on below was the 6,700-tonne steel 'umbrella' bridging the whole of Oxford Circus itself. This carried all the street traffic 1.06m above its former level. Below the Circus is a large circular ticket hall and below that are five escalator shafts, separate Victoria Line station tunnels, subways, passages and concourses linking it all together, including the Central Line at right angles.

North of Warren Street, the northbound tunnel was made to roll over the southbound to meet the needs of interchanging passengers at Euston. The reversed tunnels emerge into a combined, one-level, double-island Euston station, with the northbound tunnel on

the right and the southbound tunnel on the left. Across their respective platforms are the northbound Northern Line City branch trains to Camden Town and the southbound City trains to King's Cross. Passengers from Moorgate to Walthamstow, for instance, thus have a same-level interchange.

Beyond King's Cross, the running tunnels resume their normal positions by the southbound line crossing over the northbound.

Track

Furnishing of the line was according to the practice of the time, and used wood sleepers concreted into the roadbed to support bullhead rail, long welded into 91.4m lengths at Northumberland Park and fed into the tunnels from there. A narrow concrete shelf was affixed to the tunnel walls at platform height to contain the noise of steel wheel on steel rail. The original station decor was plain to today's eyes with grey tiling everywhere, relieved only by a motif illustrative of each station.

Automatic Train Operation

This brand-new line was an ideal opportunity to go for full automation of operation as represented by Automatic Train Operation (ATO).

Under non-automatic conditions, the train driver applies power to the traction motors, cuts it off or applies the brakes as dictated by the track and signalling conditions. With ATO, the train is under a dual system of control.

The most important system safeguards the train by employing an inductive pick-up to receive continuous coded signals from the track, with equipment on board the train to interpret and act upon these signals. No code means no movement. This is the safety signalling system. The other, the 'driver command' system, receives impulses at predetermined spots along the track. These cause power to be applied, or cut off for coasting and the brakes to be applied; a series of commands controls the stopping of trains in the station platforms.

The train operator initiates starting the train by depressing simultaneously a pair of buttons on the control desk, and operating the passenger doors. (Manual driving can be performed in the case of ATO failure.) For this he was deemed to need a clear view back along the length of his train, supplemented by closed-circuit television cameras to view from the rear. This meant straight, or nearly straight, platforms. The Victoria Line was the first application of One Person Operation on the Underground, which was a welcome gain in productivity. But overall, not using the driver as a skilled man seemed to represent rather a waste of talent.

On 7 March 1969, Her Majesty the Queen became the first reigning monarch to ride in the cab of a tube train, between Green Park and Oxford Circus, as she opened the Victoria Line.

South to Brixton

Work on extending the line a further 5km south to Brixton began in 1967, shortly before the main section to the north was opened in sections in 1968 and 1969. There are three intermediate stations.

The extension was opened in July 1971 by Princess Alexandra (Pimlico station September 1972). This brought Brixton and Walthamstow, 21km apart, within 32 minutes of each other. In its time, it was hailed as the world's most highly automated underground railway.

Shortcomings

What was wrong with the Victoria Line as built? A tunnel diameter to take surface stock was considered, but this was estimated to double the cost. Cross-platform interchange was to be adopted wherever possible, and this would have been severely constrained had that proposal been adopted. Other shortcomings were the economy measures of reduced platform widths at stations and insufficient numbers of escalators.

There was always the issue of having it imperfect, or not having it at all. If tunnel diameters had been 300mm more, the ride would have been quieter and more agreeable. The space available on the tube lines limits the design of suspension systems for comfort, and solid suspension takes up less space.

Greater London Council

The 1960s found the London Transport Board sinking slowly into deficit despite the demands of the 1962 Act for the undertaking to pay its way. This was compounded by growing staff shortages and industrial relations problems. The Greater London Council (GLC) had been created in 1963, and was complaining

Below: The 1960 stock was put to use on the Woodford-Hainault Central line shuttle service, where it served as the guinea pig for Automatic Train Operation on the Victoria Line. A four-car train with two intermediate trailers of 1938 stock arrives from Woodford at the little used Roding Valley on 3 May 1990. The station now has 49 CCTV cameras, which it is claimed works out at more than one per passenger. John Glover

that if it was to be the strategic planning authority for London, it should also have control of London Transport.

The Labour government agreed. A new London Transport Executive was set up from 1 January 1970 under the control of the GLC (Transport London Act, 1969), 'for the purposes of implementing the policies which it is the duty of the Council to develop'. Significantly, the transfer was marked by the abolition of the Transport Tribunal's functions on fares in London, with the structure and general level of fares to be determined by the GLC.

The GLC therefore became responsible for appointing the members of the Executive, establishing their general policies and approving their budgets and fares policies. The government heaved a sigh of relief; it was very much 'over to you'.

Growth hesitates

It had once seemed as if the growth in demand for travel by the Underground network would go on expanding for ever. Yet the growth was faltering. The Location of Offices Bureau did its best to encourage firms to move out of London, and by the time that the London Rail Study reported in 1974, the extensive plans and optimistic proposals for capacity increases had to be judged against a background of static traffic

levels. The growth that there was began to be taken up in the outer suburbs, with centres such as Croydon, Watford and Uxbridge bearing the brunt. And, in these, there was little or no traffic for the Underground.

Great Northern Electrics

The Northern City finally had its fate determined. From autumn 1975, Underground trains were withdrawn from the Moorgate to Finsbury Park (latterly Drayton Park) section, and the line was handed over to British Rail's Great Northern Electrics.

These services began late in 1976, connecting Moorgate with Welwyn Garden City and Hertford North. The dual-voltage Class 313 trains used 25kV ac south to Drayton Park, where they entered the tunnel section. While standing in the platform, the pantograph is lowered and the current pick-up made from the 750V dc third rail instead.

Jubilee Stage 1

The Bakerloo south from Baker Street had long been the most overcrowded of the Underground lines in Central London, and relief was planned to enhance its capacity by eliminating the junction of the Queen's Park and Stanmore lines at Baker Street. The Stanmore branch would henceforth be connected to a new Fleet

Right: *One of the most public works in the construction of the Victoria Line was the building of the underground ticket hall at Oxford Circus, which had to serve also the Central and Bakerloo lines. A massive steel 'hump' was erected in the road junction of Regent Street and Oxford Street to enable work to continue beneath it while still allowing traffic to pass. The economical note on the back of the photograph merely says 'looking west, Sunday pm', but the scale of the exercise is clear.*
Ian Allan Library

Line, from Baker Street via Bond Street and Green Park to Charing Cross (Stage I). Subsequent stages would take this to Fenchurch Street and Lewisham/New Cross Gate.

Only the first part of Stage I of what became the Jubilee line, linking Baker Street to Green Park, survives today. The regeneration of Docklands was still well into the future.

Traffic on the Underground system was falling, quite fast. The go-ahead for Stage I was obtained in 1971, with work starting the following year. When Stage I was opened in 1979, the need for the line to exist at all was being questioned. Consequently, the cost of further construction which would largely parallel the District was not favoured, while a new concept (named the River Line) arose for the further eastern projection.

Cross-platform interchange with the Bakerloo was achieved at Baker Street, and the reconstruction of the Northern line station at Strand and the Bakerloo line station at Trafalgar Square resulted in the disappearance of both those names and the appellation Charing Cross being applied to the combined station, as well as the new Jubilee line terminus.

The new part of the line was constructed with Automatic Train Operation in mind, but it was Driver Only Operation which was adopted. From its opening, the line was operated by the 1972 Mk II stock, later the purpose-built 1983 stock. A consequence of the divorce from the Bakerloo was the depriving of that line of its maintenance depot, and a new facility was built at Stonebridge Park.

On 30 April 1979, HRH Prince Charles opened the line, travelling from Charing Cross to Stanmore. The Underground's advertising advised the reader 'Get out of Charing Cross, fast!' And so the Underground did, but two decades later.

Heathrow Central

London Heathrow was officially opened in May 1946. With its air passenger traffic predicted to reach 20 million a year in 1973 (it is now over 60 million), the go-ahead for what became the first Piccadilly Line extension was received in 1971. Extra floor space for luggage was provided in the new 1973 tube stock, but with limited success when it came to avoiding impeding other passengers.

From Hounslow West the Piccadilly is extended mainly in cut-and-cover tunnel 2.91km to Hatton Cross (apart from emerging briefly into the open to cross the River Crane). From here it is in deep-level tube tunnels under the runways for the 2.09km to Heathrow Terminals 1, 2, 3. This is built in a reinforced box in the centre of the airport. The extension was opened formally by Her Majesty the Queen on 16 December 1977.

Christmas Day

Underground services had been provided every day of the year, but in the 1970s the demand for travel on Christmas Day weakened considerably. Given that it

Above: Serious and unplanned work was needed to reconstruct the railway underbridge at the bottom of Barnet Hill. It is seen here on 25 September 1969 with a 1938 stock train carefully crossing it and bound for Central London. Old infrastructure assets, and the bridge was nearly a century old at the time, need increasing care and attention. This only comes at a cost. John Glover

was also an unpopular time for staff even though it was no doubt paid at premium rates, service coverage reduced from one year to the next.

The last occasion on which such services were to be operated was on Christmas Day 1979. By then, closure of City stations was giving the District non-stop runs between Tower Hill and Embankment, missing out all the five stations in between. There were similar results elsewhere, and they would have given the opportunity for some quite exciting performances!

London Transport Museum

The London Transport Museum was opened in the former Covent Garden flower market building in 1980, replacing the earlier display at Syon Park, and at Clapham before that. Major as well as minor exhibits, many of which are mentioned in this book, are displayed here permanently.

Beyond the fringe

Travelling to some of the northern extremes of the Underground, a curious but imperceptible change took place. For this was territory outside Greater London and hence beyond the writ of the Greater London Council.

This was a peripheral area, of marginal profitability at the best of times, with both the Watford and Ongar branches having been less than successful financial ventures. Severe fares rises followed, and in the short term Blake Hall station on the Ongar branch was closed in 1981 and the rest of the service reduced to rush hours only.

Similarly, Bakerloo services were withdrawn between Stonebridge Park and Watford Junction on 24 September 1982. They were restored, to Harrow & Wealdstone only, on 4 June 1984. These events reflected capacity problems for British Rail and the Bakerloo's need for access to the new line depot at Stonebridge Park.

Fares with the GLC

The first moves away from the traditional charging methods based on distance travelled were made in 1981 with 'Fares Fair', which established a system of zonal charging on buses throughout Greater London and on the Underground in the central area. Fares within London were thus tightly controlled and when they were artificially reduced by the Greater London Council, the cost was too much for some to swallow.

It was the London Borough of Bromley whose High Court action succeeded in having the policy declared unlawful on appeal. Consequently, fares were increased by 96% in March 1982, with the result that patronage, which had been rising, took a nosedive again. Services were reduced to match the new traffic levels in December of that year.

In many ways, this was the Underground's darkest hour; from such a position, matters could only improve. Fewer than 500 million Underground passenger journeys were recorded in 1982, the lowest since 1943 when the network was much smaller and circumstances wholly different. Yet in the turmoil of the Greater London Council's fares policies for London Transport had been the introduction of zonal pricing on the Underground — a necessary precondition for what was to follow in the best-selling product of the Travelcard.

The essentials of the London Travelcard scheme were a ticket offering the holder travel by all modes on a zonal basis within a specified geographical area. It is discussed further in Chapter 9.

The original Travelcard was launched in May 1983. This date marked the introduction of the GLC's 'Balanced Plan' for transport, whereby a strategy for transport as a whole in the capital was unveiled. For London Transport this meant an overall fares reduction of 25%. The result was a restoration of the real fares level to a position midway between that before and after 'Fares Fair'. By the end of that year there were 600,000 holders of Travelcards, and passenger km

Right: It had seemed as if the Northern City Line from Moorgate to Finsbury Park, once independent and later part of the Metropolitan Railway, would never achieve its long-held objective of linking with the main-line system at Finsbury Park. This it did in 1976, and became part of British Rail. But before then it was cut back from Finsbury Park to Drayton Park in 1964, as the station platforms at Finsbury Park were wanted for the Victoria Line construction. This strip diagram displayed in tube cars shows it at its greatest extent. John Glover

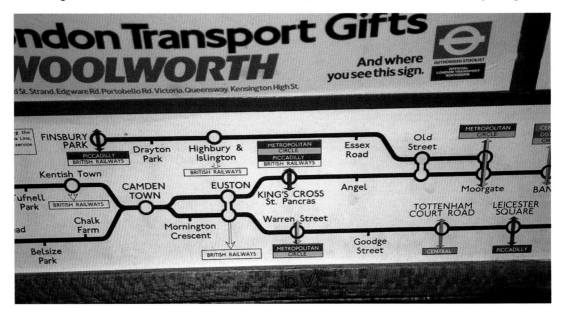

OTHER SIDE DOWN   THIS SIDE DOWN

Left: *The Northern Line had four tube stations with true island platforms, in the sense that there was nothing other than station name displays in the middle section. The platforms could become decidedly congested, and Euston was dealt with as part of the Victoria Line works. Angel, seen here in June 1990, was to remain as built for the time being. This is the view from the stairway to the platform, with a 1959 stock train for Edgware arriving.*
John Glover

travelled on the Underground rose by no less than a fifth. The number of passenger journeys made over the early 1980s reflected the fares structures; for the years 1981, 1982, 1983 and 1984/5 these were, in millions, 541, 498, 563, and 659 respectively.

Terminal 4 loop

The Heathrow Terminal 4 loop was necessary to suit changing ideas of where the Terminal would be built. Starting at Hatton Cross, trains proceeded in a clockwise direction only around this loop calling successively at Terminal 4, Terminals 1, 2, 3 and Hatton Cross again.

Flat-bottom welded rail on pre-stressed concrete sleepers made its first appearance on the tube system, while in an effort to reduce noise, sleepers on part of the new track rest on rubber fittings.

On 1 April 1986, it was opened, together with the whole of Terminal 4, by the Prince and Princess of Wales.

End of municipal control?

Following Fares Fair, the government abruptly wrenched London Transport away from the Council's control on 29 June 1984 with its London Regional Transport Act.

Although the GLC years produced some tangible results in terms of new trains and some line extensions, the whole period was characterised by the warring which took place with central government, to which the Council was often politically opposed.

GLC influence was far from consistent over the years, as administrations oscillated from one party to the other. Policy shifts are all very well, but when capital investment can last for a century or more for infrastructure and 30–40 years for rolling stock, a degree of continuity and freedom from political meddling is desirable.

Left: *The linking of a rail service – any rail service – to Heathrow Airport was a long-drawn-out affair. In the end, the Piccadilly Line of the Underground was to be the first. Ceiling panels are being installed on the platforms at Heathrow Central (now Heathrow T1.2.3) in 1977, prior to the section from Hatton Cross to the airport being opened by Her Majesty the Queen on 16 December that year.*
Ian Allan Library

5

THE MOBILE ASSETS

It is time to consider the trains operating on the system over the years, and their development. This covers matters such as construction, the source and application of electric power, performance, technical advances, internal layout and door control, and capacity.

Traditional operation

The electric motor as applied to trains for traction purposes was always of the direct current series type, and commonly mounted on the axle. Stopping has been effected by the friction of the brake shoes on the wheel treads, operated by a compressed air supply. Collector shoes which rubbed on the conductor rails picked up the traction current, which was then fed to the motors and controlled on the multiple-unit principle. Each power car picked up its own current from the live rail, and fire and insulation hazards were avoided.

All the systems had to be sufficiently developed for the whole to work, but once multiple unit control had been devised, the electric train was able to come into

Opening and closing was overseen by the guard, and interlocks detected whether each and every door was properly closed. When the door-closed circuit was complete, this would light the guard's pilot light. Only then could the starting signal be given to the driver by means of a bell. One Person Operation (OPO), of course, came rather later, but the principles did not change.

An innovation was passenger door control, which conserved heat in the open air sections that were rapidly increasing as the Underground spread out to the suburbs. Initially, this was not sufficiently reliable, and was dropped. In later years, fault detection lights were placed on the roof of each car, to alert staff to the location of door problems.

Left: *Final port of call for the pre-1938 stock from 1967 to 1991 was the Isle of Wight, where they were formed into three- and four-car trains, often to be run as seven cars. 4-VEC unit no. 041 heads a down working to Shanklin on the double-track section between Ryde St John's Road and Smallbrook Junction on 26 June 1971. These services are now operated by 1938 stock.* John Glover

its own. Thereafter, the locomotive had no place in purely urban transit systems.

In operation, the driver is concerned only with a single master controller, and the equipment does the rest. Should he lift his hand off the controller handle, the main supply to the controller is broken, current is cut off, and the brakes are applied. This is the safety device introduced in 1906 to guard against a driver's personal mishap, be it illness or collapse. The colloquial name for this part of the master controller is the 'dead man's handle'.

AC traction motors have now replaced the traditional DC type.

Door control

The use of gatemen to control entry and exit from the trains was very labour-intensive, and this hastened the search for some method of door provision and operation which could be controlled remotely. This was found in the sliding door which, when open, was recessed into a pocket in the body side. Operation was either by hand (as for many years on the surface lines) or by compressed air engine, one to each door leaf.

Standard tube stock

The all-steel clerestory-roofed 'pre-1938' stock for the tube lines was built in several batches from 1922 to 1934 to a grand total of 1,466 cars, and was the work of half a dozen different builders. Three basic types were produced, consisting of Driving Motors (DM), Trailers (T) and Control Trailers (CT).

Trailer cars lacked traction motors and compressors, but seated 48 passengers or so, unlike the Driving Motors which lost one third of their seating potential in the equipment compartment behind the cab.

The frames of the motor cars were upswept at the driving end to give clearance for the motor bogie with its 914mm-diameter wheels (all the rest were 813mm in diameter). The Control Trailers were provided with cabs and driving gear (for control) but no motors.

Formations of seven cars became general, made up M-T-T-M and used thus off-peak, with an additional CT-T-M added at peak.

A handful of cars saw further use with British Rail on the Isle of Wight from 1967 until 1989. Others became part of the engineering fleet.

Right: The Northern Line was a long-term home for the 1938 stock, which in the main served it well. A southbound train is arriving at East Finchley in April 1970; the former goods yard behind the train is now a car park, and the centre two platform roads were the route for the unfulfilled extension to, eventually, Moorgate. John Glover

Opposite bottom: Finchley Central on 5 April 1976 sees a smart train of 1959 stock arriving on a High Barnet service. This was newly arrived from the Piccadilly, and the Northern had to make do with this and other bits and pieces for the succeeding quarter century. The island platform here always looked as if it too had to manage with various temporary buildings, and it still does. John Glover

1935 stock

The 1935 experimental tube stock design was the prelude to the production run of what became known as the 1938 stock. Tube stock has been identified by a year cachet ever since.

1938 stock

The new stock offered such a boost to capacity that, in terms of seating, seven trains of 1938 stock could do the work of eight trains of Standard stock. The elimination of the equipment compartments enabled the addition of 12 seats in each of the Driving Motor cars, while the cars themselves were only fractionally longer at (typically) 15.92m instead of 15.18m.

This large fleet consisted of a total of 1,288 cars, or the equivalent of 184 seven-car trains. After the war, they formed the whole of the Bakerloo and Northern fleets, and a small proportion of the Piccadilly's. There was also modest use elsewhere.

These were the first production tube trains to use low-voltage electrical supplies for lighting and other equipment instead of the earlier system of direct supply from the current rails. Motor cars now seated 42 passengers, and additional single-leaf doors were provided. The basic seven-car formations were made up in two semi-permanent sets of DM-NDM-T-DM+DM-T-DM.

The presence of five motored cars out of seven was in recognition that multiple-unit working could also give superior performance characteristics if motors could be distributed intermediately along the length of the train to increase speed and acceleration. Such stock also had the same power/weight ratio irrespective of train length, which could thus be varied to suit the traffic on offer without altering operational performance.

The body was given a semi-streamlined appearance. A traction motor was fitted to each bogie of the five motor cars, giving a creditable 1,250kW over the whole train. Automatic coupling between sets made possible the instantaneous connection of the mechanical, electrical and pneumatic mechanism.

The last were withdrawn in 1988. Probably the most comfortable trains that have ever run on the Underground, a number were refurbished and reduced to two-car sets for use on the Isle of Wight. Six units only are now in service there, having displaced their even more elderly cousins. The whole fleet of 60-year old trains was sold by the HSBC Rolling Stock Company (ROSCO) to Stagecoach South West Trains, the operator, for the sum of £1 on 23 March 2007. There was no discount for cash.

A four-car vintage train of 1938 stock has been recreated which can be used on London Underground, but not in general service.

1956/59/60/62 stock

The 1938 stock was all built by Metropolitan Cammell or Birmingham RCW, but with the tube stock which followed, BR Derby took the place of BRCW. Following the construction of prototypes in 1956, the aluminium-bodied car with rubber suspension and fluorescent lighting became standard. Underframes remained in steel, as aluminium versions would need to be designed too large to fit the restricted space if they were to have adequate strength.

Mass produced as seven-car trains for (initially) the Piccadilly (1959 stock) and as eight-car trains for the Central (1962 stock), these cars otherwise followed closely the 1938 design. It had been intended to equip the Central line with new stock based on the 1960 Cravens design, but in the event only 12 motor cars were constructed. Some were used for the Automatic

Left: *The three trains of 1956 tube stock were prototypes of what was to become the 1959 stock. They were to be used for the Piccadilly replacements of the pre-1938 Standard stock, and were very similar in appearance. The only really noticeable change was the substitution of marker lights for the five position headcode lights on the driving ends. The train is seen here passing the entrance to South Harrow Sidings on a journey to Uxbridge, probably in the late 1950s.* Ian Allan Library

Train Operation (ATO) installation on the Woodford–Hainault line, converted to conventional One Person Operation (OPO) in 1986. These units were notable for a new type of Wedglock coupler.

The last runs of 1959 stock took place on the Northern Line on 27 January 2000, an event which also marked the final abolition of train guards.

1967 stock

The aluminium-alloy car bodies of the Victoria Line 1967 stock trains have a distinctive wrap-round windscreen, without corner pillars. The cars' primary springing was rubber, but the secondary suspension incorporated hydraulic units. Tractive power was provided by 60kW motors driving on all four axles of the driving motor cars.

For the first time headlights, as opposed to marker lights, were fitted from new. These illuminate the tunnel in front, giving the train operator some idea of the train's movement in the absence of conventional signals, of which there are few. The 1967 stock was also the first to be equipped with public address.

The oldest tube stock trains in passenger use on London Underground, they are being replaced by the 2009 stock.

Right: *The interior of a 1959 stock Driving Motor car, but this is the guard's end. The control panels can be seen, one for each side. The angled bar (right) can be raised to shut off this part of the saloon when in use by the guard, though latterly many of these fell into disuse. The location is Mill Hill East, Northern line, on 24 April 1997. John Glover*

Right: *The 1967 stock trains of the Victoria Line were rarely seen by the public in the open air, but they were prone to appear from time to time on the Woodford–Hainault ATO shuttle. On 3 October 1980 a pair of four-car units cross at Chigwell, that on the right facing east towards Hainault. The clean unpainted aluminium finish is noticeable here. It is no wonder that it was popular as a means of avoiding the cost of painting. John Glover*

1972 stock

Also built by Metro-Cammell were the very similar 1972 Mk I and Mk II designs, used originally on the Northern and Bakerloo Lines but designed for crew operation. The latter were intended for what became the Jubilee Line but now make up the Bakerloo fleet. The Mk II stock was built with red-painted doors, a first attempt to brighten up the appearance of ageing and pitted aluminium.

The former Mk I fleet has now been disbanded, with some of its vehicles incorporated in extra train sets for the Victoria and Bakerloo.

1973 stock

The 87½ new trains of 1973 tube stock delivered for the Piccadilly made provision for extra floor space for luggage to Heathrow. This was achieved by setting back the screens at the doors to offer enlarged vestibules. Car length was also increased, with the six-car train at 107m being about 5m less than the seven-car 1959 stock trains replaced and which were a little too long for the underground platforms. This had the benefit of paving the way for One Person Operation, and saved the weight and expense of a seventh set of running gear.

The Westinghouse air brake was finally omitted, and replaced by the Westcode electro-pneumatic brake. The guard's controls were repositioned from the rear saloon to the rear cab.

Experiments were also carried out with thyristor control on the Experimental Tube Train (ETT) of 1973 stock.

1983 stock

The 1983 tube stock was ordered for the Jubilee Line in two small batches totalling 31½ trains. The limitations in loading speeds caused by the single-leaf doors proved to be a problem, and the Jubilee Line extension to Stratford required more trains than this fleet could provide. The last of the 1983 cars were withdrawn in 1998.

1986 stock

The 1986 stock designs were intended as a real advance in technology. Heavy steel underframes were replaced with welded aluminium. Thyristor 'chopper' control and electric braking were both tried. What improvements could be made to ride quality, ventilation and noise levels to match rising expectations? Was full automation worth considering?

The 1986 stock consisted of three four-car prototypes. Doors were mounted externally to the aluminium body shells, and could be both opened and closed by passengers. The internal design provided more standing space and fewer seats.

The trains were given a red, blue or green colour scheme for easy identification. They provided an experimental service as six-car formations on the

Jubilee Line in 1988/9, until a derailment forced their withdrawal. One of the green Metro-Cammell cars has been preserved.

1992 stock

For the Central Line proper, 85½ 8-car trains were ordered from ABB Derby and were delivered between 1992 and 1995. A further 20 cars were ordered for (what was then) Network SouthEast's Waterloo & City line. There are three types of car, all of which are powered with every axle motored:

Type A   driving motor with cab and shoegear
Type B   non-driving motor with neither cab nor shoegear, and
Type C   non-driving motor with shoegear but no cab.

Cars are semi-permanently coupled in pairs and all types of car have automatic couplers on the outer end of each pair. All combinations of unit are fully reversible. Some are fitted with de-icing equipment.

The trains feature large curved windows in the saloon. Doors are hung externally to the body, and each pair is 314mm wider than their 1962 stock predecessors. Banishing under-seat equipment elsewhere (except for the wheels towards the ends of the cars), has allowed the longitudinal seats to be set back and thus create wider central aisles. Seating capacity is a modest 34 per car and 272 for an eight-car set. The car interior layout allows the possible rearrangement (or even removal) of seats in the centre section of the cars.

The ends of the cars have windows to enhance passenger security, and wider interconnecting doors to speed train evacuation in tunnels. Maximum speed is 105kph.

Technically, the body shell acts as a beam suspended between two bogies. The latter are of welded box-section and of Japanese origin; the suspension system is designed so that the car floor height remains constant relative to the platforms, whatever the passenger load. This is an important feature for access by the mobility impaired, but minimising the height variations helps everybody.

All axles are motored, and thyristor (chopper) control with regenerative braking is fitted. Trains have Automatic Train Control and Automatic Train Protection (ATC/ATP). This has been described as the ultimate development of the Victoria line system. CCTV is fitted in the cabs. The PA system allows the line controller to speak to the passengers as well as the driver, and a 'talk back' facility for passenger use is provided. These are 'clever' trains, with on-board performance monitoring and fault diagnostics.

Chancery Lane

It transpired though that there was a less 'clever' aspect about this stock. As a westbound train was approaching Chancery Lane station on 25 January 2003, the fifth vehicle and those behind it were derailed. The train came to a stand, partly in the platform.

The root cause was identified as gearbox failure. When the safety brackets failed as well, the traction motor became detached and fell on the track. Extensive modifications to the entire fleet meant that full services were not restored until 12 April.

It did seem that the whole costly exercise of constructing the 1986 prototypes for exhaustive evaluation had been seriously deficient.

1995 stock

These Northern Line trains are similar to the 1996 stock which in the event preceded them into service (on the Jubilee Line), though there are equipment and bogie differences. The body shells are welded aluminium extrusions. They were built by GEC-Alsthom, who had by then acquired Metro-Cammell of Birmingham.

These six-car trains of 17.8m vehicles are equipped only for One Person Operation and their introduction enabled the withdrawal of guards. They consist of two sets of three-car units, each made up DM+T+UNDM. All seating is longitudinal, but unlike the 1996 Jubilee Line stock there are tip-up seats which, in theory anyway, fold themselves up to a vertical position when vacated. They are in the area intended nominally for wheelchairs.

These cars have six automated LED scrolling visual

Right: On few parts of the system do tube and subsurface stock serve the same platforms, but one location where this is inevitable is Ealing Common. Both District and Piccadilly use the two platforms here, one en route to Ealing Broadway, the other to Rayners Lane. A westbound 1973 stock train meets an eastbound D stock train, neatly demonstrating the differences in height and floor levels of each.
John Glover

Right: The 1986 Prototype Tube stock came from three different sources, carefully colour coded so that they could be readily distinguished for market research and other purposes. The red 'C' train was built by Metro Cammell with GEC equipment, the blue 'A' train was built by BREL with Brush equipment, and the green 'C' train by Metro-Cammell with Brown Boveri equipment. Four vehicles were built of each type and they were fully compatible between types. That was just as well, since service operation required colourful trains of six cars. They are seen on 30 December 1988.
Ian Allan Library

Left: *This is the interior layout of the blue BREL/ Brush A train of 1986 stock, from which it will be seen that armrests were already doing a disappearing trick, as were any seats arranged in transverse fashion across the vehicle. The height of the window glass is a notable feature of this design.*
Ian Allan Library

display units in each, along with automated audio station announcements and a driver operable Public Address system. The Passenger Alarm offers a talkback facility with the driver.

In the cabs, the driver's seat has a control built into the armrest. A pair of small CCTV screens are built into the driver's panel, with the door controls to either side. There are steps built into the end door to allow passengers to be detrained if required rather more expeditiously than hitherto.

The 1995 stock was a scheme under the Private Finance Initiative (PFI), and the manufacturer Alsthom retained ownership of the trains. This included responsibility for their maintenance over a 20-year period, and there are opportunities to extend the contract to a total of 36 years. The trains are maintained at Golders Green and Morden as previously; both depots are now operated by Alstom. They began to enter passenger service in 1998.

The contract is performance-related and the reliability target includes a failure rate of 1 in 30,500 km (compared with 1 in 4,000 km for the outgoing fleet). There is also a 'small payment' related to the number of passengers carried on the Northern. The rental payment to LUL is expected to amount to between £40 million and £45 million a year.

Thus LUL entered into a 'power by the hour' usage contract, with a substantial element of risk transferred to the private sector. Each day, Alstom as the service

provider must deliver a fleet of reliable, clean trains which are returned to it at night. Non-availability or performance shortfalls are reflected in the usage payments.

1996 stock

The trains for the Jubilee Line as built by GEC-Alsthom had six cars per train, each comprising two three-car units. Of these, four cars are powered. The 59 trains which emerged as the 1996 stock were assembled at Washwood Heath in Birmingham (the former Metro-Cammell works), with components sourced from Spain, Canada and France. At the end of 2005, an additional trailer car was added to each train and the fleet itself was increased by a further four trains, making the fleet up to 63 seven-car units.

The trains were equipped for conventional One Person Operation with Tripcock Train Protection, but also for Automatic Train Operation or manual train operation with transmission-based Automatic Train Protection.

These trains are similar to the 1995 stock. From the passenger's viewpoint, the main difference is in the seating, as the Jubilee units have merely a place to rest one's bottom at the outer ends of the centre section of each car, as opposed to the tip-up seats on the 1995 stock. Appearance is outwardly similar to the trains on the Northern.

Right: *The 1992 stock was built by BREL at their Derby works, the bodies of which are seen here under construction. This was a large order, which was to stretch to 700 vehicles in all. These were to provide 85½ 8-car trains for the Central line, plus another five 4-car trains for the Waterloo & City which was then part of BR.* Ian Allan Library

Right: *The 1996 stock on the Jubilee line is provided with standbacks at the outside doors to try and make standing passengers less of an obstruction to those joining and alighting. The trick lies in deciding exactly how much space to allow for this. The trains were still new when this picture was taken on 24 December 1999 at Stratford.* John Glover

Left: *Longitudinal bench-type seats except at the extreme ends of the F stock vehicles and very ample standing room in the centre of the cars were an ideal recipe for moving large numbers. It would be interesting to know how they were viewed by the passengers from Uxbridge, whose journeys to London would take half-an-hour or more. Providing for a variety of needs within a single vehicle type is never easy at the best of times.*
Ian Allan Library

Left: *The F stock spent its final years on the Uxbridge services, and a train of this stock with the very distinctive oval windows is seen here at Neasden. Introduced on these trains were the no-maintenance mercury-type door interlocks, which ensured that the doors were properly closed before the guard could give the starting signal to the driver. The F stock ran until 1963.*
Electrail Collection
(4402)

2009 stock

Construction was underway in 2009 of these Victoria Line trains by Bombardier at Derby, and a total of 47 trains replaces the former 43. All should be in service by mid-2011 and at 133.2m for an 8-car train are in total three metres longer than the 1967 cars that they replace. This enables them to make use of the 'spare' platform length provided on the Victoria Line, when the accuracy of ATO stopping was still uncertain.

Nominally two four-car units, they are in effect semi-permanently coupled; uncoupling requires positioning over a pit. Each unit consists of three motored and one trailer car; doors are standard and the internal arrangements consist of all-longitudinal seats in rows of six, with two seats on each side in the centre bays being of the tip-up variety. A complete train, therefore, has 256 ordinary seats and 32 tip-ups.

THE MOBILE ASSETS

Subsurface lines T stock

In about 1923, the Metropolitan Railway converted some of their steam stock into motor coaches and regrouped the trailers into multiple unit trains. The conversion was carried out by Metropolitan Vickers and led to the introduction of the new T stock. These were the versatile 'brown' Underground trains, which retained that colour for the whole of their long operational lives. The control equipment was situated in a separate compartment behind the cab and not underfloor.

Batches appeared over the years until 1933. They were used on the Watford services, but latterly the T stock also worked to Amersham, made up into six-car and eight-car trains. Each had two motor cars.

F stock

A remarkable series of 100 all-steel cars was built for the District by the Metropolitan Carriage & Wagon Co in 1920/21. Known as the F stock but nicknamed 'Tanks', these high performance trains had three pairs of hand-operated double doors on each bodyside, and were adept at clearing huge crowds. In appearance, the 'Tanks' differed from previous and subsequent offerings, for they were fitted with elliptical roofs capped with six large ventilators and two oval-shaped windows placed at each end of all cars. At 2,921mm, the bodies were 279mm wider than previous trains, as a result of which there was an inward slope of the body above the waistline.

In the 1950s, the class found a new home on the Metropolitan services to Uxbridge. Here, they were able to exploit their power. They later became a test-bed for braking systems, and were fitted with air doors. Final withdrawals took place in 1963.

Q stock

Apart from the F stock, the characteristic American appearance of District stock was perpetuated, particularly the clerestory and the straight sided bodies with large windows. Latterly running under the generic name of Q stock, this class was built as separate sub-groups between 1923 and 1935. They were built with sliding doors, originally hand-operated on the earlier types, but all fitted for compressed air operation by 1939.

The last of the Q stock was withdrawn in 1971, its final appearance being on the East London Line.

O and P stock

The 1935 re-equipment programme enabled the replacement of elderly surface as well as tube stock. Three classes of basically similar specification were purchased: O stock cars for the Hammersmith & City, P stock for the Metropolitan, and Q38 stock for the District. A total of 573 cars was ordered from the Gloucester and Birmingham companies, of which 287

were motor cars. However, the trailers were built with conversion to motor cars in mind should the installation of extra power be considered worthwhile later.

The elliptical roofs, flush fitting windows and flared body panels, gave the cars an extremely sleek appearance. Fittings varied, and were dictated mainly by compatibility considerations with existing stock.

All motor cars were equipped with two motors rated at 113kW each, one to each bogie. Car bodies were 15.58m long, and seated 40 passengers.

The last examples were withdrawn in 1981.

R stock

Unusually, this District stock was built in several batches, starting with what became the R38 stock, then the R47, R49 and R59 deliveries. Some of these were not new at the time, but conversions from earlier builds.

Similar in general appearance to the Q38 stock, the new cars were all powered with a single 82kW nose-suspended traction motor in each of their two bogies. There were thus no trailers. They were fitted throughout with fluorescent lighting. The Birmingham, Gloucester and Metro-Cammell companies were all involved.

The R49 and later batches had lightweight aluminium bodies, saving about six tonnes per car compared with the steel versions. Early aluminium cars were painted red, but eventually all were turned out in a 'silver' livery to match the later unpainted versions.

The R stock survived in service until 1983.

A stock

The surface stock remaining to be considered was still in service in 2009, but replacement was imminent. All have been made suitable for OPO.

The A stock was delivered from 1961, to provide a total replacement for the Metropolitan Line in conjunction with the Amersham electrification. Built by Cravens of Sheffield, the A60 order was for 248 cars in four-car units, followed by an order for 216 identical A62 cars for the Uxbridge services.

Two driving motor cars sandwiched two trailers, and the performance was specified to match that of the previous stock. The traction motors were controlled for either a high acceleration rate but low balancing speed, suitable for in-town station spacing of 800m or so, or a lower rate with a different motor field strength to take full advantage of the longer outer sections beyond Baker Street. Here, the trains could indulge in 96 kph running.

The A stock was built to the maximum width possible of 2,946mm and this made 3+2 seating each side of a central gangway practicable. The width allowed for each seat was 445mm. The standard eight-car formation seated 464 plus 916 standing (total 1,380).

To overcome the loss of heat as the doors opened

up in the Chilterns on a frosty morning, the saloons were provided with extra-powerful heaters.

Conversion to OPO was completed in 1986. This work comprised the relocation of the guard's panels in the driving cabs, the fitting of public address, train radio, new windscreen wipers and toughened glass in cabs, and twin headlights.

C stock

The C stock was again built in two batches. The C69 series of 351/3 trains of six cars each was for the Hammersmith & City and Circle. Ordered in 1968 from Metro-Cammell, it was delivered 1970/71. The second batch, designated C77 and consisting of 11 trains for the Edgware Road–Wimbledon service, appeared in 1977.

Designed for quick loading and unloading, these cars featured four pairs of double doors along each side of a car body only 14.93m long. As built, there were only 32 transverse seats, arranged 2+2 in each car. Later, this was changed to 32 longitudinal seats. Unusually, all passenger accommodation is identical; the cab in the driving motor cars merely adds an extra 1.09m to the length of those vehicles. Bogie centres were adjusted to minimise overhang on curves.

These trains were constructed of two-car units (M+T) with one cab, three of which would form a service train. Automatic couplers are fitted at all unit outer ends. Among their new features was rheostatic braking as on the contemporary 1967 stock tube cars, a secondary suspension system of rubber-air springing units, and thermostat-controlled blower-heater fans mounted in the roof. A selective door-close facility enables all but one pair of doors in each car to be kept closed at terminals in cold weather. These trains pioneered manual, as opposed to automatic, One Person Operation on the Underground in 1984/85.

D stock

Only three main unit types provided the whole of the surface stock requirements for the District and Metropolitan Lines. The 75 six-car all-aluminium D stock trains made their début from Metro-Cammell in 1980. A total of 65 eastward facing and 65 westward facing three-car single cab units were built (DM-T-UNDM), together with 20 double cab-units with automatic couplers at both ends (DM-T-DM).

Four doors on each car side were again provided, but this time of single leaf only and thus 1,067mm wide as opposed to the 1,370mm or so with double doors.

Innovations included coil spring suspension supported by rubber cushions, and motor and wheelset interchangeability with the 1973 tube stock. Traction brake controls were also new, comprising a right hand 'fore and aft' vertical lever incorporating the dead man device, instead of the previous left hand rotary operated controller.

Left: Two single-car units maintained the Acton Town–South Acton shuttle service until its closure on 28 February 1959. A pair of G class motor cars of 1923 were converted to double cabs in 1939 and made suitable for operation by one member of staff. This undated view was taken at Acton Town. Ian Allan Library

Right: *An ex-LMS Class '8F'
2-8-0 No. 48166 heads a
train of new rolling stock for
London Transport through
Harrow & Wealdstone on
the up slow line on 16 April
1952. The cars were part of
the order for R49 stock
and were being delivered
from the Birmingham
manufacturer, Metro-
Cammell. All these cars had
aluminium bodies, but one
only was left in unpainted
aluminium to see the effects
of wear and to gauge public
reaction. R. E. Wilson*

Right: *A train of 'unpainted'
R stock was formed up in
1953 to run as such, with
the adornment of a red
waistband. This was later
revised so that the front
dropped down as seen here.
The styling was thus similar
to that adopted by British
Railways for their early diesel
multiple units with 'speed
whiskers'. This R stock train
forms an Ealing Broadway
working at Earl's Court, date
unknown. Ian Allan Library*

Seating is mainly longitudinal, with concealed fans in the ceilings. The D stock has proved most successful.

S stock

The new rolling stock for the subsurface lines is all of a single family of air-conditioned vehicles. Testing was carried out by Metronet on the Old Dalby Test Track in Leicestershire, formerly run by British Rail.

The S stock cars are each 16.75m long. The disruption to acquisitions under the PPP caused by the problems with Metronet have resulted in changes. Seat provision and the number of cars making up the sets shown may see revisions. The number of seats in a car can be changed by altering the proportion of longitudinal to transverse, at the expense of some loss of standing room:

S stock trains are to be eight cars on the Metropolitan and seven cars on the other lines, though the services worked by C stock might be six cars only initially.

An 8-car S stock train is 133.68m long, compared with 131.47m for an 8-car A stock. This S stock will have 256 seats (mixture of transverse in facing bays and longitudinal) plus 50 tip-ups; by comparison the A stock has 448.

A 7-car S stock train is 117.45m long, compared with 94.36m for a 6-car C stock and 100.90m for D stock. A 7-car S stock train will have 212 seats (all longitudinal) plus 44 tip-ups, the C stock has 192 seats and the D stock 280.

Depot accommodation and some platform lengths on C stock services are a considerable constraint on the use of 7-car S stock trains, but reducing these to 6 cars (and 100m in length) may cause capacity problems. In all cases, the S stock has considerably greater standing capacity than its predecessors.

The revised S stock programme under TfL is shown below and assumes the 7-car option for the C stock fleet replacements.

Use	Formation	No. vehicles	Delivery
Metropolitan	58 x 8	464	2009–11
Circle/H&C	53 x 7	371	2011–13
District	80 x 7	560	2013–15
Total vehicles		**1,395**	

THE MOBILE ASSETS

The total of 1,395 vehicles is that announced on 1 April 2008 after negotiations with the rolling-stock builders Bombardier, and was associated with taking Metronet out of administration.

The S stock trains are being introduced for manual driving with tripcock protection; ATO will come later. There are compatibility issues for ATO and the Ealing Common section which is shared with the Piccadilly Line, and similarly on the Richmond and Wimbledon branches where tracks are shared with National Rail operations. Even getting in and out of Neasden depot can cause interface problems with the Jubilee Line ATO.

Refurbishment

Rolling stock refurbishment was a main occupation of the 1990s. There were two main reasons for this.

First, safety. In the aftermath of the King's Cross fire, a general review disclosed a number of changes which were desirable. These included:

elimination of non-essential use of combustible materials in car interiors or in equipment.

revising the emergency brake alarm system to alert the driver, but not to cause an automatic brake application between stations.

speed control after a driver has had to pass a signal at danger under the Rules, whether because of signal failure or other reason.

the fitting of public address to all rolling stock.

the fitting of high intensity headlights to make trains more visible to staff on the track, and 'correct side door enable' or, to interpret, a transmission/reception device between the

lineside and the driving cab which allows the driver to open a train's doors on the platform side only.

The second reason was image; Underground trains have a long life. Seating layouts for what became the Metropolitan A stock were being tried out as a works mock-up in 1939 and as a series of in-service experiments from 1946. The A stock entered service between 1961 and 1963, and refurbishment of what were basically sound vehicles has enabled them to remain in service until well into the present century.

Tastes have changed over time. So too have perceptions of personal safety, whether this is justified or not. Research showed much support for providing windows in the car ends to improve visibility through the train, lighting enhancements, a reworking of seating and handrail positions, and a new design of upholstery.

External painting of trains began in 1988, resulting in a new corporate livery. This was aimed at offering a much improved appearance over pitted aluminium. It would also be easier to clean if attacked by the spray can. The new external finishes complemented the interior refurbishment programmes.

Work was completed on the last fleet to be refurbished, the D stock, in 2009.

Waterloo & City

Although not then forming part of the system owned by London Underground, developments on the Waterloo & City tube line are recorded here for the sake of completeness. When the original rolling stock became due for renewal in 1940, English Electric supplied 28 diminutive vehicles which were only 14.3m long and 2,635mm wide. Maximum speed was 64kph on the 5min journey between the two stations. Normal

Right: The C stock trains have done well; they are just the right sort of approach where the majority of the passengers are making short journeys. Four sets of double doors on each side of each car makes for very quick loading and unloading. But it also means fewer seats (32 per car), lots of standing room, and plenty of opportunity for cold (or even wet) journeys when the weather so decides at exposed station platforms. This is Farringdon on 22 April 2009 with an eastbound train arriving. The platforms on the left are used by Thameslink. As can be seen, they have already been extended once to cater for 8-car trains; further work is being concentrated at the other end of the platforms to allow 12-car operation. John Glover

Left: *An aluminium-bodied train in good clean condition as seen here takes some beating. This is an A stock unit forming a service to Aldgate as it passes through Neasden at speed in May 1988. The later onset of spray painting by vandals left marks which were difficult to clean off, and even then they tended to leave a shadow. In that way, the corporate livery was born.* John Glover

formation was two motor cars sandwiching three trailers, and current supplies were altered from centre third to the standard Southern Railway outside third rail.

Their drab appearance was markedly improved by the application of Network SouthEast livery. By a considerable margin, these Class 487 cars were the oldest operational trains in the London area at the time of their withdrawal in 1993.

They were replaced by a minor variant of the 1992 Central Line stock, from which five four-car trains can be made up. The line was also converted from third to fourth rail electrification. The whole passed to London Underground in April 1994.

Interchangeability

Besides the obvious incompatibility of surface and tube stock, preventing the former running on the lines of the latter (though not vice versa), there are many other factors limiting the spheres of operation of each.

Platform lengths are one consideration, with only the Central and Victoria lines able to take 8-car trains. There is also the problem of differing floor heights and hence stepping distances. Less obviously, the line depots and sidings are also unlikely to accommodate trains longer than those normally used. The Metropolitan's A stock is also too wide to be able to scrape round the Circle.

The movement of the 1972 tube stock between lines has been noted, but physical dimensions are not the only consideration. Increasingly, a technical limitation is the provision of advanced signalling systems, using equipment which is specific to each line.

Full interchangeability is perhaps of little real significance. Stock mixtures on individual lines also bring problems such as crew and maintenance staff-training, spares provision and general incompatibility.

The new S stock trains for the subsurface lines are aimed to achieve the greatest level of standardisation yet seen.

Aims of new stock

Metronet, then responsible for both the S stock trains and the 2009 stock for the Victoria line, suggested what the aims of new rolling stock should be.

First, it should be designed for easy maintenance, minimum downtime and lower maintenance costs. It will also be energy efficient and use solid-state propulsion systems which are highly reliable. These will offer significant improvement in reliability.

More motorised axles will give faster journey times and higher performance, while wide doors with stand-back areas and interiors designed to improve boarding and alighting will help keep dwell times short. They will also offer the passenger improved ventilation, lighting and ride quality.

New trains will use hard-wearing and vandal-resistant materials and finishes, providing long-lasting exterior and interior environments within extremely strong, crash-resistant vehicle structures.

Further changes

Besides the deliveries already under way, a new fleet of 92 trains for the Piccadilly Line will be in place in 2014, though those for the Bakerloo will not be delivered until 2020. Further advances in tube stock design may be expected by then. It is estimated that a further 19 trains will be required by 2020 for the Northern Line upgrade part 2.

Half-life refurbishment will be due for the Central, Northern, Jubilee and Waterloo & City fleets in 2017; by then they will soon be becoming the oldest vehicles in the fleet.

6

STATIONS AND TICKETING

The station is the passenger access point to the system, and also a place to change trains. There are a total of 270 served currently by the Underground. Of these, a handful are managed by Train Operating Companies. The total of Underground stations is a little elastic; for instance, how many are there in the Bank/Monument complex?

Which lines have the most stations? The top four are the District (60), Piccadilly (53), Northern (50) and Central (49). At the lower end are the Victoria Line (16) and the Waterloo & City (2). This, however, is far from the whole story, as usage patterns and passenger volumes are also very different.

Geographical split

The Underground is the predominant means of rail transport in central London, but its influence lessens as distances increase. Nearly half of all Underground stations are in Zones 1 and 2, or as far out as North Greenwich, Hampstead, North Acton and Clapham South. Another influence is the Thames, and the importance of the former Southern Railway electrified lines. London Underground serves only 29 stations south of the river.

Barriers, passages, circulating areas and escalators must have roughly equivalent capacity if bottlenecks are not to form; the inability to clear an area into which an escalator disgorges is a particular danger.

Similarly, there must be a means to shut off platforms to prevent them from becoming overcrowded. Closed-circuit television controlled from an operations room can be useful for surveillance, while public address is helpful. One Person Operation has long been in force throughout the system, and this requires suitable back-up systems.

Left: *Like other companies, the District Railway built many of its stations to a standard pattern, though few now remain. This is the building at South Harrow on 26 April 2008 on the eastbound side of the line. It is no longer used for passenger purposes, but is still very much as built.* John Glover

Station design

Station design and construction and, frequently, subsequent modification has to accommodate the varying traffic needs of the individual locations. If it fails in this, it fails completely.

The simplest arrangement is a single platform. At the other end of the scale, the busiest stations such as Victoria, Oxford Circus, Liverpool Street, King's Cross St Pancras, Waterloo, and Piccadilly Circus, will see between 30 million and 60 million passengers joining or alighting there each year. These Underground stations serve up to five lines, and with only four platforms in the case of three of them. They are large premises. Thus Oxford Circus has 14 escalators, 25 stairways, and 8.8km of platforms and subways.

Operational issues

Operationally, conflicting flows of passengers must be kept separated as far as possible. It is also desirable to maintain as many entrances and exits from the premises consistent with acceptable staffing levels. There must also be space for people to buy tickets.

Passenger information

Good clear directional signing for passengers is most important. Underground platforms usually carry a comprehensive notice of stations served directly opposite the point where a passenger arrives on the platform. Line and system diagrams are everywhere, and illuminated signs referring to exits, as rather than interchanges, are colour-coded in yellow.

Destination indicators which show subsequent trains are of great value to passengers, especially on lines where there are a number of divergent routes. At Leicester Square northbound Northern line platform, for instance, it is very important for many passengers to know if the approaching train is bound for Edgware, High Barnet or Mill Hill East. Where there is only one route, as for example on the Victoria line, the only variation is whether the train is going the whole length of the route.

The widely installed dot-matrix indicators show at least the next three trains, their destinations and their estimated arrival times.

Good information brings user confidence, provided it is also accurate.

Right: *Some suburban stations have unexpected traffics. At North Ealing, the afternoon peace in March 2003 is suddenly disturbed by large numbers of school-children flooding onto the station platforms. A west-bound train has recently left, an eastbound train of 1973 stock is arriving. As always, trains have the ability to move large numbers of people, very quickly. For this group, most journeys are likely to be relatively short, and the availability of seats is not likely to be a relevant consideration.* John Glover

Station modernisation

Many stations have been reconstructed or built anew on a different site. This work entails the most complicated of all Underground engineering when such items as subways, sewers, mains and even tunnels may have to be stopped up, diverted or otherwise accommodated. Engineers have not only these things to consider, but they must always make provision in their plans for the continuing daily traffic.

Station modernisation has absorbed large chunks of funds. The work is difficult as it has to be carried out around times when trains are still running and the station is in use. Consequently, much of the retiling and platform resurfacing can only be done at night or during periods of extended line closure. There were also unforeseen hazards; it was a materials store being used by a contractor during station modernisation at Oxford Circus in 1984 which caught fire and wrecked the northbound Victoria Line platform.

A wide variety of schemes has been tried; one of the most successful was that at Baker Street on the original 1863 Metropolitan and Circle platforms. The original station was lit by gas at night, but by day natural daylight came from the shafts above the platforms which had been installed to allow the escape of smoke from the locomotives. Later, accumulated grime, advertising hoardings and fluorescent lighting made it a dismal place indeed. The refurbishment involved stone cleaning, the introduction of artificial daylight through sodium lights in the old shafts, and new seats and fittings.

Other notable past refurbishments have been David Gentleman's mural of the mediaeval craftsmen building the original Eleanor Cross above at Charing Cross (Northern), and a complementary portrayal of some of the treasures of the National Gallery and the National Portrait Gallery on the Bakerloo platforms. Eduardo Paolozzi's unique hi-fi-inspired mosaics at Tottenham Court Road, the British Museum theme at Holborn, and the Brunel tunnelling shields at Paddington are

Right: *The wayside station of Totteridge & Whetstone on the Northern Line retains all its original canopies and fixtures at platform level, though the station building in the distance and on the bridge above is rather disappointing. A 1995 stock train arrives for High Barnet on 23 July 2009.* John Glover

others which catch the eye. Throughout, fittings such as cable ducts and seats are in the line colour, and standard roundel-style station names are used. Various experiments have taken place with signing.

PPP station works

Work carried out at stations may be of three main types. There is the full station upgrade meaning major works. Station refurbishment is much more limited, being a package of works to ensure that there is no serious decline in the station's condition. Enhanced refurbishment is aimed also at enhancing its atmosphere and surroundings, and reducing future maintenance needs. Each is assessed individually.

It was intended that a total of 68 stations would be step-free between street and platform level by 2010.

DC lines

The stations formerly operated by Silverlink and served also by the Bakerloo line from Queen's Park to Harrow & Wealdstone (but not Willesden Junction) passed to London Underground in November 2007. According to TfL: 'These are in a poor state of repair and don't have many of the features expected at TfL sites'. They are now being upgraded at TfL's expense.

Station congestion

The relief of station congestion then produced a list which included Monument (District) and Bank (Northern), both as a result of the DLR extension, and Goodge Street as a result of UTS. The problems vary between locations; lift or escalator capacity (eg Russell Square), the ticket barrier or ticket hall capacity (eg Bayswater, High Street Kensington), platform capacity (eg Liverpool Street, Central and Victoria, Victoria line). At Euston Square, consideration was being given to 'double-ending' the station by providing a ticket hall at each end of the platforms; here that would have the additional advantage of improving the access to Euston Network Rail station.

At Tottenham Court Road, better street access was needed, and a new escalator shaft. A total of 25 or so stations were classified as having a measurable problem, while an eye to future expansion as a result of new lines was also important. Thus a rebuilt Tottenham Court Road would ideally include embryonic provision for both Crossrail and the Chelsea–Hackney lines. But how can planners judge whether both or even one of them would be built in advance of the decision being taken?

The difficulties at Victoria were complex. The Victoria line ticket hall needed enlargement, with augmentation to the escalators and the lower concourse. Restricted platform widths increased station stop times, which had serious implications for the train service which could be operated. If trains are halted by up to a minute to allow passengers to alight and board (preferably in that order!), this constrained the number of trains per hour which could be run on the whole line. The possible solutions, all of which were exceedingly costly, included widened station platforms, additional platforms, and 'double-ending' the station.

In such cases, and Liverpool Street Central Line was as bad, the aim must be to control station stop times, and if this needed new track layouts, rolling stock modifications, staff training or signalling changes, these had to be built into the plans.

King's Cross St Pancras

One major example of station reconstruction is King's Cross St Pancras. This is the best connected station on London Underground, to the extent that it is served by six Underground lines and two major National Railways termini, as well as Thameslink.

Left: *Canopies protect the passenger from inclement weather, apart perhaps from driving rain or snow. They are even more effective when they reach the dimensions of this example at High Street Kensington. They are, however, another maintenance liability, and they need cleaning. This canopy is on the outer rail platform of the Circle Line service and the picture was taken on 11 July 2007.* John Glover

Above: The Morden extension of what is now the Northern Line was undertaken together with the task of rebuilding of the City & South London Railway and extending the Charing Cross branch to Waterloo and Kennington. It was opened in 1926. The new (as opposed to the reconstructed) stations were built from Portland stone to a similar general pattern, adapted to the constraints of the site in question. Thus there might be a relatively shallow curve in the street as here at Colliers Wood, it might be much sharper, or completely linear. They all formed part of the work of Charles Holden. This view was taken on 22 April 2008. John Glover

Below: The new Uxbridge station was opened in 1938 and is seen here in an undated photograph with a Metropolitan train for Baker Street ready to depart. The ticket barrier staff seem to be keeping a stern eye on the photographer. Notably, in those days before automatic barriers, it was deemed necessary to have three staff on duty even in the middle part of the evening. The clock says 21:18. Ian Allan Library

St Pancras is now also the terminal for Eurostar services, while the upgrading of Thameslink with a new station in tunnel on the west side of and below St Pancras is part of the scheme to much enhance that line's capacity.

The original tube ticket hall was far too small, while the steps to the ticket hall for the subsurface lines and the general layout were far from ideal. The Underground station suffered also in that it was not possible for passengers to move between the two ticket halls without exiting and re-entering the system through the automatic ticket gates. The intervening area formed part of a subway used by the public to cross the Euston Road.

Comprehensive updating and extension was the only answer, and this was tackled as follows:

- Enlargement of existing tube ticket hall.
- New ticket hall, in part below St Pancras forecourt and in part below Euston Road.
- New ticket hall on suburban side of King's Cross, north of the Great Northern Hotel (deferred, but now open).
- New access routes to all lines, including new escalators.
- New lifts to ease mobility access.
- New public subway under the Euston Road.
- New links from the Underground to both main-line stations.
- New Station Operations Room.

This massive scheme involved partial closures to many roads, including the repositioning of King's Cross

Left: *The Underground has long been good at informing passengers of the services provided on reaching the platforms; this comprehensive display may have been found at Liverpool Street for the Metropolitan and Circle lines in 1987. But times change. Since then, the Hammersmith & City line has been created, the bay Platform 3 has been removed, Wood Lane station has opened and Shepherd's Bush is now Shepherd's Bush Market. The Circle goes to Hammersmith and not to High Street Kensington without a change, British Rail is no more and King's Cross St Pancras is now also an interchange for Eurostar. This indicates how much can change over (in this case) about 20 years. Keeping enamel boards like this up to date is a painstaking and often quite costly job.* John Glover

Left: *This is the driver's-eye view when approaching Platform 1 at High Barnet in the 1960s. This has all the essential attributes of a Great Northern station, with goods sidings on the left. Only the fourth rail electrification, a 1938 stock train for Morden via Charing Cross awaiting departure from Platform 2, and the London Transport station signs suggest that this is no longer a branch terminus on the main line railways.* Colour-Rail LT281

taxi rank, and the cordoning off of areas to create temporary construction and work sites. Train services also had to be interrupted from time to time, especially at weekends.

At the same time, major railway works were progressing at St Pancras itself, while King's Cross Thameslink platforms were repositioned at low level within St Pancras.

Engineering closures

The restriction on services such as those outlined above which saw no trains between Baker Street and Aldgate/Aldgate East for a long succession of weekends in 2003 is becoming more prevalent. For instance, over Easter Bank Holiday 2009, services were withdrawn as follows (whole weekend from Friday 10 – Monday 13 April unless otherwise stated:

Circle: No service on the entire line.
District: No Embankment to Upminster, or (Friday only) Wimbledon Park to Wimbledon.
Jubilee: No service Neasden to Stratford (but services restored Waterloo to Stratford on Saturday only, after 1530).
Metropolitan: No service Wembley Park to Uxbridge/Northwood.
Northern: No service East Finchley to High Barnet/Mill Hill East and Northern line trains (only) not stopping at King's Cross St Pancras.
Waterloo & City: No service.

Station works may also cause partial or total closures, with escalator and/or lift renewals being the most common causes.

Underground services may be replaced by bus route(s) laid on for the purpose, or by stepping up the frequency on all or part of existing route(s). Three separate replacement routes took the place of the Jubilee line services above. Alternatively, passengers can be left to their own devices.

The scale of work occasioned by the infrastructure PPPs has meant that such closures are now commonplace, and that this will continue. The following extract is from a book published in 1862, discussing the Metropolitan Railway a year before the first section opened:

> 'These works ... will give employment to many, and be a nuisance to others, as long as they are being constructed. But when the mess is cleared up and the new channels (of railway) are thrown open, a sense of comfort and relief will be felt throughout the vast general traffic of London.'

Below: Separation of passenger flows to the maximum extent possible is nearly always helpful, though compliance even with simple and straightforward instructions is not always what it might be. Here at Plaistow there is no ambiguity about which side to ascend the steps, with the dark blue signing showing that it dates from the days of 40 years ago and more when the station was owned by British Railways Eastern Region. It was still there on 23 July 2009. John Glover

Right: This is the south end of Harrow-on-the-Hill station, looking north on 29 April 2009. It shows the treatment provided by Charles Holden with the rounded canopies and, in this instance, the rather severe blockhouse look of the main building. An A stock train (left) is departing for Uxbridge, and another is arriving with a service for Aldgate. John Glover

Lifts

Originally, platform access was by stairs, since the platforms were no more than 5m or so below street level. Even today, Sloane Square is distinctly unusual in having up escalators installed on both platforms. The building of the deep-level tube lines, however, demanded some form of mechanically assisted access. Initially this meant lifts, and by 1907 there were 249 lifts on the growing Underground system.

Although lift numbers decreased slowly for many years, with 60 remaining in service in 1994, the combination of new stations as a result of line extensions and a more positive approach to those with mobility problems has seen their numbers grow again. At the end of 2008, a total of 133 were in service at 54 locations.

Escalators

Lifts needed staffing, while the interruption of the flow of passengers could lead to long waiting times. Hence the search for some form of continuous movement. The first escalator was patented by a Mr Reno and installed in New York in 1894. The Otis Seeberger design became the first to appear on the Underground system at Earl's Court in 1911.

In general, it was found that two escalators could do the work of five lifts, and a 30° gradient became the standard. For the record, the greatest vertical rise can now be found at Angel (27.5m). The shortest is at Stratford (4.1m). The maximum number found together is five, at Canary Wharf.

At a speed of 44m/min, a single escalator can handle 10,000 passengers an hour comfortably. Lesser speeds

to conserve energy at times of light traffic may also be set.

Safety devices include plungers for emergency use, and these will stop the escalator in about 1.2m; these activate the brakes, which will also operate if the electricity supply fails. Detectors are also installed to stop the machine should a drive chain break.

The substitution of lifts by escalators from the 1920s found that the slope required by an escalator shaft would not join the existing ticket office with the existing below ground passages. Typically, the remedy was to construct a new surface ticket hall underneath a road intersection. Escalator shafts from there lead to landings above tube level since the tracks are generally too closely spaced to allow direct access to platforms. A short stairway joins the two.

Since then, few stations in the central area have had more than a series of subway entrances to mark their presence. This kind of work is tremendously expensive and disruptive.

At the beginning of 2009, a total of 412 escalators were in service at 83 different station locations.

Left: *This indicator is clearly from a past era, but the meaning is clear. It is to be found at Chalfont & Latimer station, but probably not for much longer. If S stock trains cannot be divided, they will be too long for the bay platform here anyway. Thus all branch trains will need to originate from elsewhere.* John Glover

Left: *This long London, Tilbury & Southend Railway seat is on the eastbound platform at the attractive District Line Plaistow station, where it continues to serve its purpose for the present owners, London Underground. It is 23 July 2009.* John Glover

STATIONS AND TICKETING

Flooding

The water table under London is rising, and with it comes the increased risk of flooding of the system. Exceptional rainfall or the breaching of water supply or sewerage pipes can also result in the discharge of water into the Underground. Without a satisfactory means of dealing with water, the Underground would quickly resemble one massive sump.

About 700 pumps are installed at 350 sites throughout the system. This includes a key installation next to the westbound Circle and District Line platform at Victoria, which deals with up to 5.5 million litres of water in a 24hr period. It is only constant attention that keeps the Underground as remarkably dry as it is.

Ventilation

A problem as old as Underground railways themselves is that of ventilating the tunnels adequately with economy, and without causing discomfort to passengers or creating nuisance for residents near ventilation shafts.

Standard practice has been to exhaust spent and heated air from the tunnels by means of powerful fans discharging into special ducts, and to admit fresh air through station entrances and escalator shafts. Fresh air is also pumped through shafts enclosed in staircase wells, or through shafts sunk specially for the purpose. A further aim has been to keep the air temperatures in the Underground at a reasonable level. Heat is created faster than it is dissipated through the tunnel segments

and into the surrounding clay, and a series of fans has helped to stabilise the temperature underground.

This, however, has not been enough. More frequent Underground services, increasing demand and heavier high-performance trains all generate more heat so, without additional measures, temperatures will rise further. This also has an effect on asset performance and reliability.

The air-cooling of new subsurface stock cannot be applied to the deep-level tube lines. These are much more constrained for space, and any proposed system has to take that into account. The problem is, however, being tackled, with the three areas being on board the trains themselves, the running tunnels, and the platforms (plus the rest of the station as well). In each case, there is the problem not only of the method of cooling, but the practical means of ridding the system of the unwanted heat.

Left: *One of the most impressive flights of escalators can be seen at Canary Wharf, between the ticket office level and the main station entrance. This is the view on 19 February 2003 from the lower landing. The lighting introduced into the panels at the side of the escalator steps is a recent innovation and still relatively uncommon.* John Glover

Left: *The passimeter booking office was much used in the 1930s by both London Transport and the LNER. The idea was that at less busy stations, tickets could be issued by the clerk on one side, and collected by him on the other. Optionally, the gates could be controlled by the clerk. Later they fell out of favour on the grounds of security, but they were also completely incompatible with the requirements of the Underground Ticketing System.* Real Photos/ Ian Allan Library

STATIONS AND TICKETING

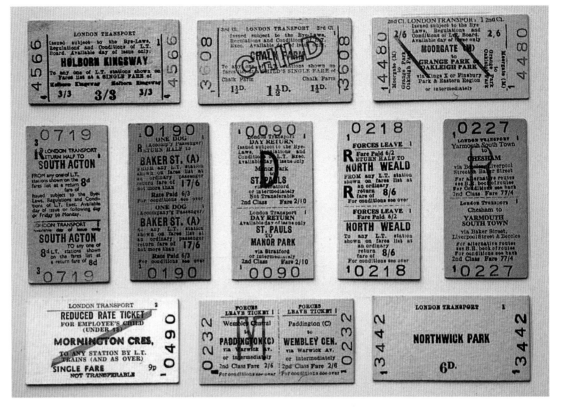

Below: These Underground tickets are all post-decimal machine issues. From left to right, then top to bottom they are: Uxbridge adult cheap day return to any station at a single fare of £1.20, total fare paid £1.70; Hillingdon adult single to any station at a single fare of 80p (from Ultimatic dispenser); Blackhorse Road adult return at single fare of £1.30, total fare paid £2.60; Tottenham Hale adult single to a BR destination at a fare of 80p (yellow oxide-backed ticket); Paddington adult machine-issued single at a fare of £1.60; King's Cross adult privilege single at a fare of 10p. John Glover

Above: These Underground tickets are all pre-decimal Edmondson card issues, or before 15 February 1971. Note that 12 pennies (d) make 1 shilling (5p) and 20 shillings equal £1. The fare of 77s 4d is thus £3.87 in today's coinage. From left to right, then top to bottom, they are: Holborn adult single to any station at a fare of 3s 3d, dated 14 AU 67; Chalk Farm child single at a fare of 1d, dated 25 FE 56; Moorgate adult single to Grange Park or Oakleigh Park (via King's Cross or Finsbury Park & Eastern Region) at a fare of 2s 6d; South Acton adult return to any station at a fare of 8d; Baker Street dog return to any station at an adult return fare of 17s 6d, (but fare paid for dog 6s 3d); St Paul's to Manor Park adult day return via Stratford and BR at a fare of 2s 10d; North Weald Forces Leave return monthly fare of 8s 6d (but fare paid 6s 2d); Chesham to Yarmouth South Town via Baker Street, Liverpool Street and Beccles adult return at a fare of 77s 4d (valid 3 months); Mornington Crescent employee child under 18 single at a fare of 9d; Paddington to Wembley Central via Warwick Avenue, Forces Leave return monthly fare of 2s 6d; Northwick Park adult single to any station at a fare of 6d, dated 14 NO 68. John Glover

The comprehensive upgrades to the Victoria and Piccadilly Lines include planned cooling programmes.

Tickets

A ticket represents the means by which an acknowledgement is given by the railway for a fare tendered, and confers on the passenger an authority to travel. It follows that the ticket and the means of obtaining it are all-important parts of the organisation. Besides being a more-or-less foolproof way of collecting revenue, tickets provide a record of where a passenger entered the system. Without a ticket or an equivalent, such as an Oystercard or Travelcard, it is

not possible to charge fares graduated by distance, which is a severe limitation.

A busy system

What has always distinguished the Underground from the main-line railways was the sheer volume of journeys made. In 1875, with less than 16 route km of track, the Metropolitan was calculated as issuing 20% more tickets than the whole of the Great Western Railway. With the proliferation of through booked tickets ensuing after 1907, the situation quickly became untenable, given also the number of stations on the network and the possibility of different classes of travel.

This culminated in the gradual introduction of so-called 'scheme' tickets from 1911, when all stations available at a given fare were listed on the back of the ticket instead of requiring separate prints for each.

Mechanisation of ticket issue by the 'Rapidprinter' machines which printed, dated, guillotined and ejected a ticket on the press of a button by the ticket clerk arrived in the late 1920s. By then, the Underground Group was issuing around 270 million tickets a year. Passenger-operated machines followed, together with help for change giving.

The 1950s saw the introduction of the 'Station of Origin' ticket, which conferred the right to travel for any journey from the originating station to any other where the fare was that shown on the face of the ticket.

Electronic ticketing

Ticket gates were first installed at Stamford Brook in 1964 as a prelude to their use on the Victoria Line. This somewhat breathless and curiously dated description of the gating of the latter is taken verbatim from a London Transport advertisement of 1969:

Open Sesame. From the passengers' point of view perhaps the most novel feature of all is the electronic gates in the ticket halls. Now when you buy a ticket you show it to a machine which sucks it in, scans it, and releases a barrier for you - in about a third of a second. And when you leave a station a similar gate takes your ticket from you (always assuming you've got the correct ticket) and lets you out, returning your ticket if it's a season.

This magic has an electronic origin. The special yellow tickets are backed with magnetic tape on which are recorded the details of your journey. The idea is to save you, the passenger, money, because it reduces hard-to-come-by station staff - and will deter fare dodgers. And if the gates seem strange at first you'll find you get used to them pretty quickly.

Then you can look forward to inviting country cousins up to town, to demonstrate quite casually your mastery of modern electronics.

Underground Ticketing System

Sadly, the requirements had not been properly thought through and the system fell into relative disuse. What amounted to the rebirth of automatic ticketing came in the 1980s, with the Underground Ticketing System (UTS). The objective had now expanded to improve the control and issue of tickets and security for the staff. It also represented a return to first principles; the previous systems had developed gradually from the early days, and modernisation had always been piecemeal. The main features of the new system were:

* Self-service ticket machines which issue a wide range of daily tickets and give change.
* Automatic ticket checking on entry and exit at Central London (Zone 1) stations, in which 80% of all journeys start or finish.
* Creation of 'open' no-barrier suburban stations without regular ticket checks, but with more roving inspectors able to levy penalty fares.
* Secure 'wall' ticket offices for staff; all machines can be serviced without leaving the office.
* Data-capture to provide centralised accounting reports and management information.

A credit-card sized ticket was adopted as standard, with a magnetic strip on the back for encoded data.

Left: *Ticket issuing for the Victoria Line broke new ground. Despite the new National Cash Register machines shown in this photograph, the racks of Edmondson tickets for the less common issues are still well filled. The dating press and the (empty) change-giving machine with the shaped tray into which this discharges are prominent in the unoccupied window position. Very quick service and making it easy for the passenger are all important.* Ian Allan Library

Left: *The ticket hall at Victoria, probably around 1975, shows the stand-alone ticket machines and a ticket hall rather less busy than it often is today.* Author's collection

STATIONS AND TICKETING

Encoding takes place on issue, together with visual printing of the station at which issued, fare paid and other details.

The design of the automatic gates installed in the central zone uses a 'paddle' system, in which the paddles are kept closed electro-pneumatically. Tickets have to be inserted and collected from another slot before the gates will open; photo-electric cells detect the presence of a passenger so that the gates remain open while the passenger passes through. The gates open automatically in the event of power failure, or by the operation of emergency buttons. The minimum number of gates at any one station is one inward, one outward and one reversible gate. At busy stations such as Oxford Circus as many as 26 gates were installed, replacing a maximum of 10 manned booths.

Installation was completed in 1989, and linked to the compatible British Rail system. UTS featured many enhancements over what had been intended previously, such are the advances in micro-electronics.

It took less than a second for gates to perform 64 checks and rewrite the magnetic stripe. Thus the new ticket readers were able to detect irregularities in ticket use through time, history, geography and price tests. The acid test, though, was its acceptance by the public and the staff who had to use and run the system respectively. This was achieved and eventually UTS became all but universal.

Oyster

The revolution in transport ticketing and revenue collection represented by the Oyster card is now all but complete. Worldwide, more and more operators are recognising the benefits of contactless Smartcard technology, and hard practical experience on an increasing scale is now being added to the theoretical case.

This contract was let in 1998 to TranSys Ltd, who developed a new revenue collection service for London Underground, London Buses, London Trams and the Docklands Light Railway under the Private Finance Initiative. TranSys financed and provided the operating system. There are many opportunities for expanding the system and this includes the various Train Operating Companies in the London area.

Smartcard is like a credit card that contains a small micro-chip (a memory) which can process and store electronic data. It is attached to an aerial inside the card; when the card reader reads the card, power flows through the aerial and information moves from the card to the reader and back again. Reading is achieved by the card being 'shown' to the reader, which needs to be within only a few centimetres of the card; the latter does not leave the customer's possession. The result has been the quicker passage of customers

Below: The Victoria Line saw the introduction of automatic ticket gates, but not for those with ordinary green tickets, thank you. This is Vauxhall station on 16 March 1983 in the early stages of the revised ticketing arrangements. John Glover

Right: The standard station entrance nowadays has a line of UTS barriers which can seem mildly intimidating, a little-used ticket office window and (out of this picture) a bank of ticket machines. This is Harrow & Wealdstone on 28 June 2008. Keeping access to the gates available to everyone at all times can cause a few problems. John Glover

through the gates, with the reduction in the 'fumble factor'.

An Oyster card is obtained by the holder making a down payment and the card is given an equivalent value. This is encoded on the card. Each time the card is used, the value remaining is reduced by the amount of the fare charged for the journey. The card can be topped up at any time by the holder making additional payments at a ticket office, and these are also encoded. The card itself thus continues in use for an indefinite period.

Stored Value Ticketing

This whole concept is known as Stored Value Ticketing (SVT). Crucial differences from the Travelcard are that the geographical area over which travel may be made is limited only by the scope of the scheme, and that each journey is charged individually. The number of fares differentials has also been reduced, and Underground cash fares for adults travelling within Greater London in 2010 are £4.00 or £4.50, or £3.50 for journeys not including Zone 1. Oyster fares are a little lower but sometimes much lower, and are generally charged at a reduced rate during the off peak. The minimum Adult Oyster fare is £1.80 in Zone 1, but £1.30 for journeys elsewhere.

This has some strange results, in that the fare (cash or Oyster) from Heathrow to central London by Underground is the same as if you travel from Heathrow to Epping, the furthest eastern extremity of the Central Line. Conversely, for cash payments, you do not pay that much less if the journey is for one station only. Such are the joys of simplified ticketing.

There is a daily price cap equal to the price of a Day Travelcard (i.e. the non-time restricted version) using the pay-as-you-go option. However, if your journeys

start after 09:30 Monday to Friday and you will also be beginning journeys during the 16:00-19:00 period, an Off-Peak Day Travelcard may be cheaper. That has no afternoon time restrictions. The age-old warning of *caveat emptor* (let the buyer beware) should never be forgotten.

It should also be mentioned that Oyster has been extended progressively to National Rail services in the London area, with fares restructured as a result.

The Oyster card can also be loaded with a period Travelcard, with validity of up to a year.

From TfL's point of view, ticket purchase and ticket validation now needs less in the way of resources, much more management information is available, and fraud should be contained more effectively. The stated overall aim is to make ticket purchase and use easier and to support the concept of integrated transport.

The responsibility for the management and development of the Oyster card system passed to Cubic Transportation Systems and EDS in 2010.

7

RUNNING THE RAILWAY

The Underground network has expanded and contracted over the years, but of a more subtle nature are the changes in the responsibilities for the trains, track and stations. These are not so immediately obvious. At present, London Underground serves 270 stations, of which 260 are operated by the company.

Visitors to Central London tend to assume that the network is indeed below ground for the most part, but as Table 7.1 shows, less than half is in some form of tunnelling:

Table 7.1: London Underground Network

Length of route owned/managed

Sub-surface cut-&-cover	32km	8%
Deep level tube	149km	37%
Below ground sub-total	181km	45%
Above ground	221km	55%
Total	**402km**	**100%**

The timetable is the written expression of the formal plan of action, which confirms what is being offered to the passenger and summarises what the organisation expects of its staff. Indirectly, it also commits the resources which are necessary to provide the service advertised. Before the timetable compilation is attempted, therefore, the volume and pattern of traffic must be known or assumed, and the resources available must be assessed.

Revision

The decision to revise a timetable may stem from a number of reasons as well as shifts in the pattern of demand sufficient to affect the service levels to be

Most of the network (88%) is double track but there are two major four-track sections, west of Barons Court on the District/Piccadilly and on the Metropolitan main line in part paralleling the Jubilee. More than one Infraco is involved in both cases. There are a few single-track sections such as the Chesham, Kensington Olympia and Mill Hill East branches, but there is also the T4 underground loop on the Piccadilly.

Sections where the Underground runs parallel to a wholly separate National Railways, such as Bromley-by-Bow to Upminster, are not included in this calculation.

Timetable planning

Few travellers on the Underground need to give any thought to the timetable, most probably assuming that trains run on some sort of continuous basis. In reality, the timetable is constructed carefully to extract the maximum out of the resources which are available. Any railway service can only be as good as its timetable, and given the things that can go wrong, the performance is usually a little below what has been planned.

provided. Technical changes involving the trains, track layouts or signalling, and the availability of staff, are all matters to which the compiler may need to address his skills. A thorough knowledge of the physical characteristics of the line, and the performance capability of rolling stock are also needed.

The journey time is the summation of the individual start-to-stop timings for the inter-station distances, with an addition for station dwell times. These need to be adjusted according to whether the period is the peak or off-peak, or whether the stop is in the central area or the suburbs. Too long an allowance and the train has to wait until its correct departure time. This results in a slow and inefficient operation, but too tight and chronic unpunctuality quickly ensues. The number of trains required to operate the service is determined by taking the round trip time plus the layover at each terminus and dividing it by the service frequency.

In putting a timetable together, the requirements at the different times of the day need to be blended with each other. It is obviously undesirable to proceed directly from a 10-minute off-peak service to a peak

Left: This simple trailing crossover is seen here at the south end of Totteridge & Whetstone station on 23 July 2009, with a 1996 stock train departing. This is sufficient for emergency use when reversing trains, but has its shortcomings. Besides making sure that all passengers have left the train before it leaves the platform, which in itself takes time, the train has to draw forward, the driver has to walk back inside to what now becomes the front cab while the points are changed and movement authority is obtained, and the train can then make the crossing movement. Meanwhile, a queue of other trains can build up, waiting for the line to be cleared. Something rather more sophisticated is needed if trains are to be reversed regularly.
John Glover

Right: *District Line travellers bound for Central London line up along the platform at Turnham Green, ready to pounce on any available seats as their D stock train arrives in February 1998. Commuters generally are very good at working out exactly where to stand to maximise their chances of a seated journey. By comparison, casual users haven't a chance!*
John Glover

frequency of perhaps two minutes between trains. Given also differential running times, the trickiest part of the job is to achieve a gradual change in frequency without causing large service gaps.

Constraints

The ability to supplement or reduce the service level depends on any physical constraints; in particular, this includes conflicting moves at junctions and waiting for platforms at termini. A basic principle is that trains should run at even intervals, but this always becomes difficult where lines diverge, as does, for instance, the Central at Leytonstone. Should the traffic so require, it is perfectly possible to run trains in a ratio of two to one destination and one to the other, but not to do this and maintain even intervals throughout.

To these sorts of problems, there are no perfect solutions. The difficulties, however, are those of mathematics rather than unresponsive or reluctant management. The best single answer, which is only feasible if the business so justifies, is to run an intensive service. One third of a 30tph service is still 10tph, or a train every six minutes. The other line has trains at 20tph, but at two- and four-minute intervals alternately.

Does the total service capacity match the demands placed upon it? If it doesn't, no amount of service tinkering will overcome this. The best that can be achieved is going to be an uneasy compromise, and will result is general dissatisfaction amongst the passengers. It might just be possible to add in another train, but at some stage this will have an unfortunate effect on the quality of performance.

Station time

For the operators, station stops are non-productive time during which the train is cluttering up the system and not earning revenue. Dwell times vary from a minimum of 15sec to 30sec or more at very busy locations. Ideally, all station stops should take an equal amount of time, but this is rarely achievable. The result is the 'bunching up' of the service, which ultimately restricts the frequency at which it can be operated.

Overall speeds also depend on the number of station stops; it was to reduce end-to-end journey times and make more productive use of trains and crews that the 'non-stopping' of trains was in vogue during the inter-war period.

Terminal requirements

The track layout at terminals is of especial significance, since trains spend longer than average at such locations. At an intermediate station, the provision of a central bay as at Putney Bridge (with platform) or Marble Arch (without) keeps the terminating train clear of the running lines.

The disadvantage of the siding beyond the platform is that it takes time to detrain all passengers and close the doors before the train can proceed, by which time another train can be waiting behind. The provision of a mere crossover to reverse trains is too restrictive for general use.

At terminals, the usual choice in tunnel is an island with crossovers (Elephant & Castle, Walthamstow Central), or on the surface a three-track multiple platform arrangement (High Barnet, Uxbridge).

Left: *The Moorgate accident of 1975 when a train ran into a dead-end tunnel and collided with the end wall at speed, with multiple casualties, resulted in many additional protection measures. This is Putney Bridge on 1 June 2009; an eastbound D stock train is arriving, while a terminating C stock train occupies the central bay platform. The very large train arrestor is seen in the middle of the picture. This has clearly been there for many years, but it is now supplemented by an approach-controlled signal, two approach-controlled 10mph trainstops along the platform, with fixed red lights and a fixed trainstop at the end of the platform.*
John Glover

RUNNING THE RAILWAY

Right: *North of Harrow-on-the-Hill are six running tracks. From right to left they are, respectively, the southbound fast, the southbound slow on which the A stock train is arriving, a reversing siding, the northbound Uxbridge, the northbound local, the southbound main (for Marylebone only) and the northbound main. The descriptions reflect the main functions each track has on leaving the station area. Thus cross platform transfers are available in each direction for Metropolitan line trains, and trains for Amersham or Aylesbury will normally leave from the same platform. There is a diveunder to take both the Uxbridge tracks beneath the two mains and the northbound local. There are also numerous crossovers at both ends of most of the six platforms, to enable trains to move between lines according to their stopping patterns.* John Glover

Platforms both sides of a track can be useful in separating arriving and departing passengers by judicious use of the door opening/door closing sequence. It can, though, make for cold trains in the winter months.

Step-back crews can be employed to hasten turnrounds. By having staff positioned ready to take the train out again after it has arrived, the time taken is not affected by the need for the incoming driver to change ends.

Limitations

Other determinants of the capacity of lines are the performance of trains, junction conflicts, signal spacing, gradients and track curvature. Nevertheless, a service frequency of 30 trains per hour should be achievable on most parts of the Underground.

Service interruptions

The then newly appointed managing director of London Underground, Tim O'Toole, was said to remark that while disruption to the service was usually recorded and the passengers were told, there was nothing to indicate when services were performing normally.

This resulted first in boards at station entrances with 'Good Service' being indicated, or otherwise as might be appropriate. Planned closures for engineering works were one reason that service provision would slip.

But like many such good ideas, events seem to have spiralled out of control. Loudspeaker announcements on a network basis to the effect that good services are operating on all (or specified) lines are now made, but sometimes these do not quite accord with reality. Thus seen from the southbound platform at Marylebone one

Right: *An unusual feature of Brent Cross was that it was furnished with outside non-platform tracks so that fast services could overtake other trains while they were in the platform. The remains of what is now no more than the trackbed (in both directions) can be seen in this northward looking view of 1 June 2009. The inter-war period laid great emphasis on speeding up journey times and South Kentish Town was a Northern Line closure for this reason in 1924.* John Glover

evening, a Bakerloo train came to a halt with the saloon lights off and no passengers on board. The driver was waiting for the signal to clear. As the indicator clearly showed that another train was 2 mins behind, this was hardly a disaster. However, the dulcet tones of the PA system then told everybody that a good service was operating.

So cynicism sets in. Passengers conclude that if nothing is being said, the service is usually operating well. If they are told that a good service is operating, that usually means that it isn't and that extended intervals – or worse – are occurring. On the other hand, if substantial delays are said to be a problem, they may well have been sorted out by the time that the information reaches the passengers.

The passengers may even be initiated into the dark secrets of railway operation: 'This train will be held here for a short time to even out the intervals in the service.' Thus a driver to passenger announcement at Hyde Park Corner one morning. On a more serious note, the one thing that needs to be avoided at all costs is passengers getting restless if a train stops between stations more than briefly, and then using their mobiles to call the emergency services.

Connections

Timetables also determine service connectional possibilities, and obvious problems arise if the services to be connected do not run at similar intervals.

The timetable also has to return the trains at the end of the day to where they will be wanted the following morning. This is not necessarily back to their starting points, since outbased trains stabling in sidings overnight have to return to depots for periodic routine examination. At intervals, they also require both internal and external cleaning.

Generally, operational control can be made more effective if services are self-contained between specific terminals where possible, such as running Arnos Grove–Rayners Lane and Cockfosters–Heathrow on the Piccadilly Line. All trains, though, should pass common crew change points.

Northern line problems

The aborted Northern line extensions, whatever benefits they might have provided, would certainly have caused major problems for the operators. The Northern would have become a complete railway in its own right, and the service provision correspondingly complex.

Today, the Northern has what might be called two and a half termini at the northern end, two routes through central London via both Charing Cross and Bank, and one (only) south from Kennington. To run a frequent service from each of High Barnet, Mill Hill East and Edgware, via both in-town routes, and for them all to proceed to Morden is just not possible. Compromises have to be made, and even then operating a reliable and regular service is far from easy. To give but one example, running all Edgware-branch trains via Bank to Morden and all High Barnet and Mill Hill East trains via Charing Cross to Kennington helps to eliminate delays as a result of conflicting moves at the junctions. On the other hand, it also creates a lot of forced interchange for people who otherwise would have a through service, especially at Camden Town.

This also has implications for station dwell times, and the likely imbalances of peak and off-peak traffic requirements on the two routes. A further serious and not easily solved complication is the imbalance of depot stabling and engineering facilities.

Left: *The countdown notices at the side of the track tell the driver how many cars have left the platform when the train pulls away from a stop. Thus, if none are left on the platform and the emergency alarms are sounded, the best course of action is usually to carry on until the next station. Providing assistance of any sort is usually much easier in locations where the doors can be opened and there is a platform alongside. This example is at Hounslow Central on the westbound Piccadilly in April 2004.*
John Glover

RUNNING THE RAILWAY

Right: *Inter-car barriers have been fitted to rolling stock generally in recent years to guard against the possibility of passengers falling between the cars. The flexible barriers are seen here on a train of D stock at West Ham on 23 May 2009.* John Glover

Late night operation

In 2000, the London Regional Passengers Committee undertook research into the services provided by the Underground and also the main-line railways late at night.

The Underground generally closes down some time after midnight, but what level of use is made of it after, say, 22:00? The 105,000 entering Zone 1 stations to begin their journeys at such times have grown substantially in recent years, and this is largely a West End phenomenon. Thus Leicester Square is responsible for 12.7% of the total.

Amongst the questions raised were:
- What is the cause of late-night travel growth, and is the trend likely to continue?
- At what time should it be possible to leave central London by train and still get home?
- Is there a case for running trains much later or even all night) as practised in some cities in other countries – though not in Britain?

The extension of the times of operation has an equal and opposite effect on the time available to carry out engineering inspections and maintenance work, which is of short enough duration already. It is, however, a fair point, which centres on what Londoners can reasonably expect their public transport system to provide.

Signalling

Signalling is the means of enabling the railway to run frequent trains at speed on potentially conflicting courses, but with safety of operation. The complexity of the signalling system is related to what is expected of it; thus the capacity of a traditionally signalled railway is dependent in part on the signal spacing, which determines the minimum gap between succeeding trains. As a safety back-up, additional devices come into play, should either the human element or a mechanical defect supervene. The most important advance in safety was the adoption of automatic signalling, whereby each train alternately protects itself and clears the road behind by making and breaking certain electrical circuits in its passage.

Above left: This basic protection device, there to stop a train which attempts to pass a signal at danger. has been used for many years. While the signal is at danger this arm is raised to the position shown. It will then strike the tripcock of any train which passes over it, and this results in a full brake application. The driver has then to reset the tripcock. From time to time it may be necessary for a train to pass over a raised tripcock (in accordance with the rules), and regular Underground travellers will be familiar with the sudden stop and exhaustion of air in the braking system which results. Usually, drivers will inform passengers if this is about to happen. John Glover

Left: When the signal is cleared, the arm moves to the lowered position, as shown, and thus will not engage the tripcock on the train. Both photographs were taken at High Street Kensington on 30 May 2009. John Glover

Left: *This is the old Metropolitan Railway signal box at Farringdon on 22 April 2009. It is situated at the west end of the station and is still extant, albeit no longer used as such.* John Glover

Below: *Signalling is a key function which keeps the trains at a safe distance from each other at all times, but it also regulates the service in terms of how frequently trains can run. In the inter-war years, the Central Line employed semaphore arms which could give three indications of stop (arm horizontal), proceed at caution (arm raised at 45 degrees), and all clear (as shown here). It thus gave similar indications to the three-aspect colour-light signal. This example is in the London Transport Museum.* John Glover

Automatic signalling

The earliest years of the twentieth century saw automatic signalling introduced on many underground lines, though colour lights (as opposed to semaphores) were not used on the above ground sections until the Edgware extension was built in August 1924. The last of the semaphores was not replaced until 1953.

Automatic signalling works as follows:
The running rails are divided into lengths which are insulated from each other electrically. The signal current passes along the rails on one side of a section of track, through a track relay, and then back through the rails on the other side. When current is flowing through the relay, its contacts are closed, and this completes the circuit for the control of the signal and causes it to show a proceed aspect.

When a train passes the starting signal and thus enters the track circuit section which the signal protects, the wheels and axles bridge the running rails and short-circuit the signal current. This de-energises the signal relay, which causes the signal to show a red aspect. When the train clears the track circuit section by passing another signal plus a further short section or overlap beyond that, the short circuit is removed. The signal relay is re-energised, and the normal green aspect of an automatic signal is restored, allowing the following train to proceed.

With several automatic sections between two signalboxes which retain non-automatic control as at junctions, trains can follow each other safely without further intervention.

Above: There are great changes coming in signalling, with the function being transferred generally from lineside indicators to cab displays and automation. This fine display of traditional signalling is at the end of Platform 2 (left) and 3 (right) at Cockfosters on the Piccadilly line. It was photographed in May 2001. John Glover

Track circuits

The track circuit depends upon the presence of a train to short-circuit the running rails.

Should a driver ignore the signal aspects, a second line of protection is brought into play. The automatic train-stop apparatus alongside the rails will apply the brakes, taking control out of the driver's hands. Normally, the arm on the train stop lies clear of the trains, but it is raised automatically by air pressure when the signal turns to a danger aspect. In this position, the arm position is pre-set to make contact with a trip cock on the train, and if contact is made the cock will open and release the compressed air supply in the train pipe and apply the brakes, causing the train to stop within the overlap distance. The raising of the train stop is detected by the preceding stop signal which will remain at danger until the fault is rectified.

This 'failsafe' approach is always apparent in railway signalling matters, and it will be realised that a loss of current in the track-circuiting device already described will always cause the signal to display a red aspect.

On the Underground system, two-aspect red/green signals are sufficient for most purposes; yellow is used as a repeater for a red aspect in advance where the sighting distance is limited. Exceptions include the sections where Underground and main-line trains use the same tracks as happens north of Harrow-on-the-Hill, where four-aspect signals provide additional braking distance.

Automatic signals cannot themselves cope with junctions, and here semi-automatic signals are installed which have to be cleared each time for the route selected, although they will restore themselves to danger automatically after the train has passed. It follows that they normally display a red aspect. Usually, such signals can be set to full automatic operation when a series of trains is to take the same route. Junction signals will normally feature the 'lunar' lights, a series of three white lights placed at an angle above the signal head as a visual indication of the route setting to the driver. Lack of any indication indicates that the 'normal' route is set.

In the mid-1950s, programme machines were introduced on the Northern line, allowing automatic route setting according to a pre-set timetable.

For slow-speed operation, the theatre-type indicator is used. This can display various numbers, each of which indicates a separate route through the illumination of a pattern of electric lamps. It will usually be found above a ground or shunt signal controlling the entrance to sidings.

Speed control

Signalling may also be used to control train speeds rather more directly than just displaying large numerals to denote speed restriction signs at the side of the track. With approach control systems, the speed of the oncoming train is assessed by the current it generates. A related relay responding only to alternating current below a given frequency is connected, and only when the relay operates does the signal clear.

Speed control of this nature allows trains to enter platforms where the signalling would normally demand that they be detained in the running tunnels as, of course, the time taken in the platforms will allow the next train in front to proceed further.

Stop and proceed

The stop and proceed rule addresses the problem of what happens when a driver encounters a signal at red and which resolutely refuses to change to a proceed aspect. In order to keep the traffic moving, this rule was devised. After a 1min interval, this allows the driver to 'trip' past it and, after resetting the trip cock on the train, to proceed at a speed consistent with stopping short of any obstruction that he may encounter or at the next signal.

The obstruction may be no more than a failed train stop which, as noted, will cause the signal behind to remain at red. However, it may be a failed train, in which case the normal procedure would be to push it until such time as it can be diverted to siding or depot. Such action minimises service disruption, but the safety of this operation does depend upon the driver of the second train continuing with care.

There have been a number of accidents when this did not happen, some with serious results. In the last analysis, no safety device can replace the skill and vigilance of the staff.

Computerisation

The inevitable move into computerisation of signalling tasks is proceeding concurrently with resignalling schemes. The first use of computers was for track circuits, and allowed the elimination of the insulation joints in running rails. These could be replaced by impedance bonds, the track circuit being tuned to a particular computer detector.

Control offices

Although signalling was originally carried out locally, supervision from some kind of control organisation, which is in a position to take a broader view of what is happening on the network was found necessary.

With a high degree of service interaction, even a quite trivial delay at one location can have consequential effects out of all proportion to its inherent significance. The problems are clearly worse when lines are being run at or near their capacity.

The example of Earl's Court on the subsurface lines shows some of the problems. In the peak hour, the westbound District line at Earl's Court has to deal with services from Embankment in the east and High Street Kensington in the north, bound for four separate destinations west of the station. In addition, there is a need to mesh in with the Circle line services in both directions, though they don't serve Earl's Court.

Above: This undated view is of a traditional signal box which uses miniature levers. There is thus no heavy manual effort, as is the case with a mechanical frame. The location is West Kensington; the signalman looks as if he has been carefully posed so that the whole frame can be seen. Real Photos/Ian Allan Library

Most but not all of the junctions are grade separated, and there are two westbound platforms available at Earl's Court itself as well as two terminal platforms at High Street Kensington. Nevertheless, given also the interfaces elsewhere with the Hammersmith & City and the Metropolitan lines, the huge scope for out of course running is apparent.

'No driver available'

Problems which fall to the controllers to deal with include those which local management has been unable to resolve, such as no driver being available to take over a train when it arrives at a crew changeover point. This can be doubly disruptive to the operation, since not only is there a potential gap in the service, but there is also a train without a driver holding up the system. Other commonplace events include train, signal and track failures, or actions by passengers or staff. The job of the controllers, who are organised on a line basis, is to keep an eye on all that is happening, and to anticipate and to minimise the effects of unwanted events on the train service. The principle is that of intervention when needed; if everything is running perfectly, the controller has nothing to do.

To undertake the control task effectively, a flow of incoming information is required, together with an intimate knowledge of the track layout, rolling-stock characteristics, station facilities, the timetable and traction and other current supplies. The objective is to minimise the causes of delay and to contain such delays as cannot be prevented to the smallest possible geographical area.

In the event of disruption, the controller has to decide on the appropriate action. This may include turning trains short of destination, ensuring train crews are available, reducing the service interval, organising a replacement bus service, calling out engineering staff and, of course, restoring the service to normal. The controller has an information assistant who can use the selective public address facility to inform passengers of operational problems, whether they be irregular running or the non-availability of lifts at a particular station. It has to be said that such public announcements are not always audible, and often seem to be largely irrelevant.

At all times, the safety of staff and passengers must take priority. For major incidents, the line controller can turn to the Headquarters Controller, who would normally summon the public emergency services.

Communication equipment

The Drico system dating from the 1950s allowed direct speech communication through speakers in the cab and the control room. Contact was made through attachment to the same tunnel wires; the train had to be stationary, and there was no facility for control to call the driver.

For the Victoria Line, carrier-wave contact through the conductor rails was used to transmit messages between the driver and the regulator. While this system could be used while the train was in motion, it suffered from interference and could not be used if short-circuiting devices had been put down after the current had been discharged. It was thus likely to be useless in the event of a real emergency when communications were most needed. The 1967 Victoria line stock was the first to be built with a public address facility.

With Driver Only Operation in mind, STORNO train radio was developed. This benefited the whole operation of the railway and provided the front-line communication between train and control. Train radio was operated by means of a continuous leaky-feeder cable through the running tunnels, transmitting to and receiving from fixed on-train equipment. Radio also allows contact with supervisory and management staff, and station staff also benefit. The provision of direct contact at all times is one of the prerequisites for driver-only operation.

The Private Finance Initiative Connect contract outsourced the provision of radio and transmission services to the Underground over a 20-year period to Citylink Telecommunications. The contract required the consortium to deliver an entirely new network-wide integrated digital radio and transmission infrastructure to replace the existing communications systems.

Copper cables have been replaced with an integrated radio system, supported by a new fibre-optic transmission system; the whole is to help staff keep in contact with each other, exchange information to co-ordinate passenger flows, and respond in case of service disruption. A side effect is that passengers are able to use mobile phones throughout the tunnelled parts of the network. Connect voice quality is much better and the system is more reliable than that which it replaced. Train drivers have hand-held receivers, which they can take with them if they need to leave the cab.

Remeasuring the railway

The railway itself is now metric, in the sense that distances are expressed in kilometres from a common base. Somewhat surprisingly this point is at Ongar, though the branch was still extant when the exercise was carried out.

Distances are denoted with posts/plates every 0.2km, proceeding westwards along the Central Line to its termini at West Ruislip (64.54km) and Ealing Broadway (54.61km) respectively. Distances on other lines are calculated via 'transfer locations', from which measurements may increase or decrease.

Thus the transfer to the District is at Mile End (33.13km) from which distances go down to Upminster (12.19km) or up to Barons Court (47.8km), where there is a transfer to the Piccadilly. Distances go down from here to Cockfosters (22.04km) and up to Heathrow Terminal 5 (69.40km). By making the transfer location Barons Court, this avoids any conflict between District and Piccadilly distances on the joint section to Acton Town and Ealing Common.

The transfer location from the Piccadilly will be found at Rayners Lane Junction (64.33km) to the Metropolitan. This subsequently avoids conflict when this too transfers to the Jubilee at Finchley Road (50.14km). Other Piccadilly transfers are to the Victoria Line at Finsbury Park and the Northern Line via the connecting link at King's Cross. The Jubilee too transfers to the Bakerloo at Baker Street.

The Central Line's transfer point to the Hainault loop is at Leytonstone (26.59km), not Woodford. From Leytonstone distances go down until reaching Woodford Junction (12.01km via Newbury Park, but still 20.84km from Ongar). Also, Stratford is at 30.3km on the Central Line, but 27.43km on the Jubilee. That reflects the whole series of transfer locations, as mentioned.

The result is that on each line there is a continuous progression that takes branches into account, but the start and finish values are only vaguely relevant. Thus the Victoria Line is measured as 48.61km at Brixton and 27.33km at Walthamstow Central (station to station distances). From that it can be worked out that the line is 21.28km long, as far as passengers are concerned.

It will be seen that the start point needs to be remote to avoid negative values occurring. It also accounts for the high value at Mantles Wood beyond Amersham, and mentioned earlier.

Left: *Communication between members of staff has always been important, and this was the loudaphone which enabled the guard (seen here) to speak to the driver, and vice versa. It was activated by pressing the button as shown and speaking into the cup. The loudspeaker for the reply is behind the grille.*
Ian Allan Library

8

MAKING IT ALL WORK

The engineering function is fundamental to the Underground. W. S. Graff Baker, then Chief Mechanical Engineer (Railways), LPTB, gave his presidential lecture to the Locomotive and Carriage Institution in 1940. In it, he defined the timeless base points for designers in engineering:

1. Will it work?
2. Is it as simple as possible?
3. Can it be maintained easily in service?
4. Can it be manufactured?
5. Does it look well?

Curiously though, the cost, whether in terms of the capital cost of equipment, the running costs or its maintenance, did not feature in his list.

This chapter takes a look at some of the many areas in which engineers contribute to the operation and safety of the system.

The term 'asset' is considered to encompass whole systems, sub-systems and components. 'Infrastructure assets' are the fixed track, signalling, electrification, plant and telecommunications equipment and structures. 'Mobile assets' cover the trains and other powered rail vehicles.

On an electrified railway, there are two main interfaces: wheel–rail, third/fourth rail–shoegear.

Both of them need to work if the train is to move. Otherwise it doesn't, and that is nowadays an important contractual matter as well as being highly exasperating for all concerned.

The purpose of the running rails themselves is to act as hard and unyielding surfaces on which steel wheels may run, without causing abrasion or rutting to either. They also act as beams to transmit the weight of the train to the sleepers, and to interact with the wheel tread and flange to guide the direction of the train.

For many years, the standard running rail on the Underground system was of 47kg/m bull-headed section in 18.3m lengths, secured by oak or steel keys to chairs in which the rail was seated, which were coach-screwed to the sleepers.

Sleepers

Wooden sleepers have many positive attributes, among them the relative ease of handling compared with the heavy concrete variety. Jarrah wood, a costly hardwood imported from Australia, was universally used in tunnel sections, with sleeper ends held in concrete to prevent track movement. Track 'creep' could, if not prevented, lead to clearances between trains and tunnels being fouled. In the open sections, creosoted fir or similar wood sleepers at rather closer intervals was the standard.

Left: The former presence of the main line railway, in this case the LNER, is discernible in this view of West Finchley with a southbound 1996 stock train arriving. Since there is no longer any need to exceed the tube loading gauge, the road bridge was lowered when it was reconstructed, thus easing its profile for road users. It is 1 June 2009. John Glover

Permanent way

The track and its support is the literal foundation of the railway: it has to be strong and resilient enough to withstand the weight, speed and frequency of rail traffic to be run upon it. It must also be sufficiently stable to offset the worst that climate and weather can do, and needs to wear well and minimise the requirements for maintenance and, ultimately, renewal. For the sake of good relations with the surrounding property owners, it must also offer reasonably unobtrusive running, particularly in terms of the noise generated.

The weakest part of the rail is at the joint with the adjoining rail, and this is always supported by closer spacing of the sleepers. However, rails become worn and are subject to cracking at joints, and rail lengths were extended. Standard rails are welded into 91m lengths at Ruislip and transported to site on trains of bogie bolster wagons. Once on site, the wagons are withdrawn and longer lengths are then welded together.

Constraints to the process include the allowance needed for rail expansion, (of little import in the tunnels as the temperature remains fairly constant),

Right: *This view of a crowded westbound platform at Mansion House station was taken on 24 September 1983, before the station was rebuilt. This was then the busiest section of the Underground, with 31 trains per hour during the peak. A C stock train is arriving on a Circle line service.*
John Glover

Right: *Sleet, snow and ice have never been friends of the fourth (or third) rail networks. One way of clearing them in the past was to use a pair of redundant tube stock motor cars, strip them internally, cut them in half and join up the two cab ends. They would then be refitted with tanks of fluid. This could then be sprayed on the conductor rails, assisted with wire brushes to scrape them clear. They were classified as Electric Sleet Locomotives. The Metropolitan main-line with its relatively steep gradients and generally exposed infrastructure was a prime user. Here is seen No ESL106 in between duties at Rickmansworth on 8 March 1970.*
G. W. Sharpe Collection
(SD102)

and the insulating joints giving electrical separation within each running rail, required for signalling purposes. For the rails themselves, flat bottom section is now standard.

Much of the trackwork is undergoing thorough renewal from the foundations upwards. Track fires in tunnels need to be eliminated, and involve more people than just the civil engineers. Such work includes:

- Screening of all ballast to clean it.
- Use of non-flammable rail lubricants.
- Eliminating the hydraulic handbrake on trains and its propensity to drip oil.
- Train-mounted transponders to detect conductor rail gaps and cut the current without sparking.
- Thermo-energy cameras on trains to measure temperature changes, and perhaps in the long term, laying fibre optic cables in the tunnels able to detect to the nearest metre local rises in temperature of 2° C.

Track geometry

What is permissible in terms of track geometry will affect the speeds attainable and the type of rolling stock which can be run. Furthermore, it is the most restrictive of the curves or junction layouts on a railway which is the determining factor. One of the advantages of a light rail system is its greater ability to accept these constraints, but for the Underground a maximum gradient of 3.3% (1 in 30), and curves of not less than 400m radius are desirable. At junctions, curvature is eased as far as possible, but space constraints in older tunnels frequently result in less than ideal situations. In any event, trains need to clear junctions as quickly as possible to keep the traffic moving, and in this sense 'clearance' is what the signalling system will accept.

Points and crossings all receive heavy wear, as the wheels passing over them deliver a series of blows. The tougher manganese steel is used in busier locations, since it is not only the capital cost but also the disruption caused by replacement or by welding repairs which justify its use. Wearing of all rails, particularly on sharp curves, may also be eased by the use of rail lubricators which use the wheels of passing trains to spread a film of grease for distances of up to half a mile.

In traditional systems, points are operated by compressed air. Movements actuated by the signalling apparatus complete a number of electrical circuits, one of which opens a valve to admit compressed air to the cylinder of an air engine placed alongside the points, and the ensuing thrust of the piston moves the point blades across. This gives rise to the characteristic 'hiss — crash', which can be observed when points are changed. Air supplies are contained in the piping which is present on the walls of running tunnels. Facing points, that is where the approaching train has the choice of route, must be locked in position to prevent their movement during the passage of the train. Those which are always trailing to the direction of traffic may be unworked, with the blades being pushed across by the leading wheels.

Tube constraints

Serviceable points and crossings are critical to the ability to run services on London Underground, and many may be in tunnel sections. Those at Camden Town and Kennington are prime examples, but there are others. On open sections of line there are usually not less than two units (as part of a crossover for instance) and these or more complex layouts can be replaced in an extended weekend possession.

In the tube lines, access is much more restricted and the geometry has already been decided by the way the tunnels were constructed in the first place. That severely limits the ability to introduce any variations. Renewals are nowadays expected to use flat-bottom rail rather than bull head, with air-operated point motors being replaced by electric ones.

Replacement is usually programmed to occupy three 52-hour shifts on successive weekends, and this introduces the need to make the track usable in between. Thus temporary arrangements have to be made, perhaps restricting the switching abilities of the normal layout, and correcting this later.

At a more basic level stopping short of full replacement, the jobs required include sleeper timber renewal, concreting to ensure stability, new rails as needed, stretcher bar renewal, replacing or attending to all fastenings and similar as required, checking for gauge, repairing or replacing joints, welding repairs to crossings, and other tasks which may present themselves. In all cases, signalling cables in particular may be disturbed, and these also have to be reinstated, checked and tested before the train service can be restored.

Above: *This stern notice is displayed at the south end of Platform 2 at Harrow-on-the-Hill, the platform used primarily for southbound Chiltern Railways trains for Marylebone. As can be seen, it isn't just a dead section. That is the end of the conductor rail, for good!* John Glover

Electrification systems

Today, the system is fourth rail at 630V DC, with the positive rail outside the running rails and the negative return in the centre. The use of the fourth rail system reduces electro-magnetic interference and stray currents, and the ability of the latter to corrode pipes and cables. The live rails on which the pick-up shoes slide have their surfaces above that of the running rails.

All the other underground lines were either built or later converted to this standard, although on the Central Line the positive rail is positioned slightly higher than normal because of constrained tunnel dimensions.

Today, variations occur where the infrastructure is shared with trains of National Rail over the following sections:
- Bakerloo line between Queen's Park and Harrow & Wealdstone.
- District line between East Putney and Wimbledon.
- District line between Gunnersbury and Richmond.

These sections have third and fourth rails with the positive outside the running rails, but the central

Right: *The acquisition by London Transport of a fleet of former Great Western Railway pannier tank 0-6-0PTs seemed almost bizarre when it took place between 1956 and 1963. Being obtained on the cheap, as it were, from British Railways, they were seen as a better bet than costly new battery locomotives. This is No. L90, though it is not known whether it was the first or the second locomotive to bear that number.* Author's collection

Below: *The pannier tanks which were owned by London Transport for a time mostly found their way to preserved railways. One such was No. L99, (BR No. 7715), built by Kerr, Stuart & Co. in 1930. Seen here in steam at the Buckinghamshire Railway Centre at Quainton Road on 13 April 1998 with a train of British Railways coaches. The locomotive is still in the fine maroon livery favoured by its second owner, several shades darker than that favoured by BR for coaching stock.* John Glover

negative rail is provided solely for the benefit of Underground trains and is earthed to the running rails. To the casual observer, they appear no different.

A disadvantage of using relatively low voltage dc traction current is the need for frequent substations by the lineside. The heavy currents involved and the cost of equipment were among the reasons that British Railways eventually adopted ac overhead traction supplies in the 1950s, but clearances in any case would have been insufficient in the Underground tunnels.

The new subsurface S stock trains are designed to run on 750v dc if the power supply is upgraded from 630v dc. This would increase the power to weight ratio and offer potential energy savings.

Conductor rails

The function of the conductor rail is to enable the moving train to collect traction current which is generated in a fixed substation. On the train, it is fed to the traction motors via the control system.

Top side contact conductor rails as used on the Underground were of 64.5kg/m rectangular section in tube tunnels, and 74.4kg/m flat-bottomed section elsewhere. They are made from low-carbon steel. The outer conductor rail carries the positive traction current, and will be found on the side furthest from the station platform wherever possible; the centre conductor is the return. Both are, of necessity, supported on insulators.

Potentially, aluminium conductor rails offer lower electrical resistance and hence less waste of power.

The fourth-rail system is not without its problems; old tunnels can be wet, in which case they are likely to deposit muck on the conductor rail from above. Ice is also a well-known problem; when the temperature hovers around freezing, it produces freezing fog and arcing. The difficulty with oil-based de-icing fluids is that they cause rail damage and reduce conductivity; oil is poor at transferring current and causes arcing. It is electrical wear, rather than mechanical wear, which is the primary difficulty.

Arcs can also be caused by gaps in the conductor rail, as at pointwork. They result in damage to both the pick-up shoe and the rail. Whose responsibility is the damage? Are good rails being wrecked by the shoegear, or is it vice versa?

Despite the above, the fourth-rail dc system has worked superbly well. Its only real operational vices for urban applications are the susceptibility to frost and snow, and the potential safety hazard.

Physical connections

Apart from those joint sections of line listed above, there are a few other locations where Underground trains may proceed to and from Network Rail infrastructure. These are at West Ruislip, to give access between Ruislip depot and the Chiltern line, which is not used for passenger purposes, and at Harrow South Junction (towards Marylebone) and Mantles Wood, north of Amersham (towards Aylesbury), which stem

from that being part of the former Great Central and Metropolitan Joint operation. A recently introduced connection is that at Barking, using which trains may run from the Tottenham & Hampstead Network Rail line onto the eastbound District tracks. This too is for engineering train usage.

There are, however, physical connections between all the Underground lines with the sole exception of the Waterloo & City, which is completely self-contained. In the past, this facility was provided for access to and from Acton Works, and is now used primarily for the movement of engineering trains.

These routes are often of considerable length, and may require reversal(s). This has implications both for the time taken and for line occupancy. Thus a journey from Lillie Bridge depot (west of Earl's Court, District Line) to (say) Epping requires running via Ealing Broadway and reversal, while to reach Golders Green requires running to Hammersmith (reversal), King's Cross (reversal) and thence direct to destination.

Operation of the subsurface lines involves much inter-running between them, with many connections in the vicinity of the Circle. However, the availability of a route does not necessarily imply that it is available to all types of train and the D stock, for instance, is not permitted to run north of High Street Kensington.

Lillie Bridge and Ruislip

Track maintenance nowadays is highly mechanised, and the main depot for the whole of the Underground system is at Lillie Bridge, west of Earl's Court. Despite

Below: *Electric traction is durable, and the vehicles with their electric motors can outlive their usefulness from the passenger's point of view. Thus old cars find a new lease of life in the engineering fleet. Here a pair of pilot cars, nos L130/L131, are seen at Acton Works on 3 July 1983. They were used for ferrying other vehicles around the system as required.*
John Glover

MAKING IT ALL WORK

Right: *Flange lubrication with some kind of oil/grease compound will ease the passage of wheels around sharp curves and reduce the associated squeal that this manoeuvre makes. It does, however, have the propensity to spread the mixture other than where it is really wanted.* John Glover

Right: *Fulham Bridge used by the railway is seen here from Putney (road) Bridge. This is a very substantial structure, though it still suffered serious damage when it was rammed by a barge some years ago. The picture shows it being crossed by a C stock train travelling from the north bank (left) towards the south bank (right), and thence on to Wimbledon. It is 29 April 2009. From the passenger's point of view, the bridge girders block a view of the river, the converse of which is that not much of the train is visible from elsewhere.* John Glover

space limitations, it is well situated at the geographical centre of the system which minimises the valuable time taken to run works trains in non-traffic hours.

Remodelling of the premises has provided a new points and crossings workshop, a new railway track layout to separate road and rail movements in the depot, the rationalisation of storage facilities and the installation of a new maintenance area for battery locomotives.

Rail welding is carried out at Ruislip. Flash butt welding consists of placing the rail butts, or ends, together, and passing high tension current through them. The rails are drawn apart slightly during the operation to create an arc, and when this has been done a few times the butt becomes so hot and soft that when pressed tightly together they fuse into one.

Track machines and cranage

A fleet of wagons for track maintenance purposes is retained. These include ballast hoppers and flat wagons for carrying pre-assembled sections of track. Of interest are the specialist vehicles, which include four cranes. The movement of a crane to any part of the

Underground system imposes severe design limitations if it is to negotiate tube tunnels successfully. .

A five-car tunnel-cleaning train was built at Acton in the 1970s, and acts as a giant vacuum cleaner in tube tunnels during non-traffic hours.

A fleet of tamping and lining machines from the Austrian firm of Plasser and Theurer carries out by machine tasks that a few years ago were left to careful observation and measurement followed by hard physical work.

To find out where this work is most needed, a Track Recording Train entered service in 1987. It consists of an instrumented 1973 stock trailer, specially modified by British Rail at Derby, between two 1960 stock pilot cars. Other pilot cars for ballast trains and moving trains or parts of trains around the system other than under their own power are formed from old passenger driving motor cars.

Traction for haulage

Traction for engineers' trains was provided by the fleet of retained steam locomotives after passenger train haulage passed to the LNER in 1937. In 1957, the Underground acquired two steam Pannier Tank locomotives from British Railways, renumbered them and painted them in lined maroon livery, setting them to work on miscellaneous duties. A maximum of 11 was later in service at any one time. They were finally withdrawn in 1971, being replaced by three Sentinel diesels (themselves now defunct) and more battery locomotives.

Most haulage on the tube lines is now provided by the battery locomotive fleet, usually placed one at each end of their trains to speed reversal. All are of tube-loading gauge to enable them to pass anywhere without restraint, and have variable-height drawgear to suit both tube and surface stock coupling heights. Wherever possible they operate on current obtained from the conductor rail, during which time the batteries (on the more modern locomotives) are recharged in readiness for use where no live supply exists. Charging time is about 1hr for each hour of discharge. There is a fleet of 32 such locomotives; built by various manufacturers over the last 50 years. They cost about £2.5 million each.

In some years, winter weather precautions are hardly needed. Sleet locomotives were used to help in solving the current collection problems during winter weather by the use of antifreeze solution, liquid sprayers and wire brushes on the conductor rails. These locomotives have now been replaced by equipment on a number of passenger cars.

New approach

More intensive track renewals under the PPP requires the use of extra capacity. Use is now made of trains to and from Network Rail on the subsurface lines which can accommodate them, with access as recorded above. A new contract is held by GB Railfreight and

Tube Lines (as the party responsible for the engineering train fleet) for the provision and haulage of track components to and from site. Nine Class 66 locomotives have been acquired, together with around 160 wagons of various descriptions.

On a weekend possession, the first engineering train will remove the track and the next three will take out the old ballast. The following two will bring in the new ballast, followed by another with sleepers and rail. The last provides the top ballast. Separate arrangements are made for tools and small component delivery and the subsequent collection of tools and scrap.

Operation is mainly from a distribution base at Wellingborough, Northants, where the trains can be stabled. Materials from various sources such as sleepers and lengths of rail are stockpiled here; the site is equipped with gantry cranes. Ballast comes from the Isle of Grain.

Autumn leaves

The autumn has always brought the problem of falling leaves, and various methods of removing them before they are ground to a slithery paste on the rail have been tried. This included water cannon, but in 1983 a Unimog tractor and trailer which could run on road or

Left: *Engineering work often means the provision of bus replacement services, and these too have to be signed in some way. This is the way they are being shown outside Hounslow West station in May 2004, and similar additions to bus stops are now commonplace.*
John Glover

rail was acquired to vacuum up the leaves as they fell. This unit was kept at Chalfont & Latimer station high in the Chilterns, where many of the worst problems are to be found, and made night time sorties. However, it was found that Unimogs could not be relied upon to operate track circuits at all times; this is a serious deficiency on vehicles intended for use on the running lines. This and two later acquisitions were later restricted to depot shunting purposes only.

Work on the infrastructure

In practical terms, very little infrastructure work can be achieved when passenger trains are running. The prime time for this work is thus during the night hours, which are strictly limited.

On the London Underground network, every part of the system is designated either as part of the Line-Clear Area or part of the Line-Safe Area. This excludes non-electrified track, and that within depots and sidings where traction current is normally switched on at all times. In general, the Line-Clear Areas include all sections of line where clearances are very severely restricted, as well as those in tunnel (tube or otherwise). Line-Clear Areas include for instance the whole of the Circle line, and the Northern line south of the East Finchley/Golders Green tunnel mouths, but also the Burroughs Tunnels at Hendon. The Line Safe Areas refer to the rest of the system.

Each day is divided into Traffic Hours, during which traction current is switched on, and Engineering Hours when current is switched off. The times at which Engineering Hours begin and end vary according to location and day of the week. Roundly, Engineering Hours cover the period from 01.00 to 05.00 on Monday nights/Tuesday mornings to Friday nights/Saturday mornings, 01.00 to 06.00 on Saturday nights/Sunday mornings and 00.30 to 05.00 on Sunday nights/Monday mornings.

In the Line-Clear Areas, access for engineering activity of any sort, including routine inspections, may be made only within Engineering Hours. In the Line-Safe Areas, minor activities which do not affect the safety of the trains may be undertaken within Traffic Hours, subject to making suitable staff protection arrangements.

The exceptions are the undertaking of major works, such as bridge reconstruction. Realistically, these cannot be achieved within a series of night-time occupations, and must be undertaken as one continuous job over (say) a weekend. In such cases, extended Engineer's Possessions are arranged specially, and bus replacement services or similar are provided for passengers.

The short time available for engineering work, and the unsocial hours during which it must be carried out, means that it is costly. It is also difficult to make full use of labour during the limited hours available on each shift. Getting men, equipment and materials to work sites can only be achieved after the traction current has been switched off. This accentuates the importance of

optimising the pathing of Engineer's trains from Lillie Bridge, Ruislip and Neasden. There is a need:

To allow maximum time at the site concerned to avoid delaying the start of (or imposing an early finish on) other scheduled engineering work on the route which they need to traverse, and not to affect the operation of passenger trains.

Staff and equipment

It will be seen that the problem is not merely that of funding and the commitment of resources, but also the limited opportunities available to use them productively. This has in turn led to a rather more protracted series of line closures than would take place in an ideal world.

The upkeep of ageing infrastructure is a major problem. The use of low-maintenance forms of track and other assets is a sensible step in the right direction, but the key difficulty is the lack of sufficient Engineering Hours during the course of the day.

While the relentless pursuit of efficiency will continue to make a necessary and welcome contribution, market projections envisage an increasingly busy Underground system as the years progress. But this also means more wear and tear, irrespective of any outstanding backlog of maintenance work.

One possible solution is to reduce Traffic Hours by perhaps an hour every night, with a corresponding increase in Engineering Hours, but this is not what the customers want. There are also the effects on traffic revenues to be considered. There would not seem to be any end to weekend or longer-period closures for the foreseeable future.

Power generation

The early tube railways began the tradition of self-sufficiency in power generation and built their own power stations. The electrification of the Metropolitan and the Metropolitan District Railways spawned coal-fired power stations at Neasden and at Lots Road, Chelsea respectively, in 1905. By this time, the District and three of the tube railways were under the unified control of Yerkes, and Lots Road which was then claimed to be the biggest power station in the world, provided power for them all.

A review of long-term requirements and the cost of running power stations came to the view that Lots Road should be decommissioned. This formed part of a Private Finance Initiative deal in August 1998 between what is now EDF Energy Powerlink (EPL) and London Underground. EPL operates, maintains, finances and renews the Underground's high-voltage power distribution network under a 30-year contract worth more than £1bn.

Under the terms of the deal, EPL is required to complete a major programme of capital works, which included the installation of equipment to provide emergency supplies to the railway in case of a major

Opposite top: *Ballast Motor L148 (1938 stock ex 10022) was photographed at the Bakerloo's London Road depot in March 1979 when it was about to perform a duty on the last stores train. The overall reddish-brown livery did not enhance the livery of service stock, and it certainly didn't make it any more visible to those working on the track when it approached.* Colour-Rail (LT58)

Opposite bottom: *Ruislip is a major line depot and seen here on 15 March 1997 is a 1962 stock Driving Motor being lifted, and a 1992 stock DM No. 1630 along-side. This view gives an idea of the volume of work which can (and needs to be) undertaken on line premises.* John Glover

MAKING IT ALL WORK

Above: *This is the weed-killing train formed of 1938 former Ballast Motor Cars nos. L150 and L151 at Ruislip depot on 17 March 1997, in pristine condition. Weedkilling is something which needs to be tackled on a regular basis, in particular to prevent the ballast from becoming clogged and hence failing to drain properly.*
John Glover

power failure, replacement of existing power control systems, and renewal of the Northern's power distribution system. The company is also responsible for distributing high voltage electricity supplies to every Underground station and 400km of track. London Underground's payment is made on the basis of an availability charged for the services provided.

The contract is also designed to deliver major power supply upgrades which will support the PPP enhancements.

Lots Road power station was switched off formally on 21 October 2002, following which all Underground power was derived from the National Grid. Supplies are delivered to the Powerlink network at the bulk supply points of Lots Road and Aldgate, together with an existing point at Neasden. Back-up battery systems installed at the stations are capable of powering emergency lighting, PA systems and train radio.

Greenwich has been retained but restricted to providing emergency cover. Four gas turbines at Greenwich are supposed to be sufficient to counter a total power failure in southeast England. They can be brought into use within a quarter of an hour to take over from the batteries and to provide power for tunnel and station lighting, ventilation, pumps, lifts and escalators. This allows passengers to be evacuated from tunnels; but there is insufficient power to provide for traction purposes.

However, none of this was able to prevent a 34-minute power loss over more than half the Underground system on 28 August 2003, following National Grid failure.

Substations

The function of substation equipment is to receive high tension current, step it down to the traction voltage, and rectify the supply from alternating current as generated to direct current at 630V as required by the traction motors. The current then flows through track feeders to the conductor rail, each length of which is bonded or welded to its neighbour to minimise voltage drop.

Over the whole Underground system there are approximately 100 substations which are either part of London Underground or, in some cases, Network Rail. The substations are unmanned, and use mercury arc or silicon rectifiers. Current can be cut by the operation of relays in the substation which trip the track breakers; all stations have the facility to do this in emergency, as have train drivers when underground by pinching together the tunnel wires.

Each section of track is fed by the substation at each end (double end feed), apart from terminal sections (single end feed). Electrified sections are discrete, and separated from each other by gaps in the conductor rails; in the event of a failure a section can be neutralised without affecting nearby parts of the line. If a section in advance of an approaching train is dead, a triangle of three red warning lights alerts the driver to an approaching train. The driver should attempt to stop short or, if this is not possible, to ensure his train is completely on the dead section. Otherwise, he will bridge the section gap and render the section in advance live, which could endanger persons on the track or otherwise exacerbate the incident which caused the current to be discharged in the first place. Substations also provide current for ventilating fans, lifts, escalators, lighting and pumps.

Power electronics

Power electronics for rolling stock offer tremendous potential. The positive effects include energy saving, regenerative braking, jerk-free operation, wheelslip control, elimination of fire hazards through doing away with dc starting resistances, response to supply variations, and no contactor maintenance. Conversely, they add weight, interact with signalling and power supply, and need a greater engineering input.

Similarly, there are huge gains to be made in the interrelated fields of signalling, traffic control, communications and passenger information. What could be more antiquated in concept than traditional block signalling when track capacity is the most precious asset? Computer-aided engineering enables calculations on matters such as safety and immunisation to be made more accurately. This, therefore, reduces the likelihood of wasteful over-engineering. Simulation for site-specific designs can be carried out, and the testing of trade-offs. The need to build prototypes for engineering reasons has now largely passed.

Another fast-developing field includes management information systems; the instant calculating ability of computer systems vastly enhances the capability of flexible systems scheduling. The concomitant need is for wholly satisfactory agreements to be reached with the staff.

The sheer scale of potential technology impacts must be managed, with London Underground determining where it is going and organising itself accordingly. Engineers determine standards. Equipment procurers (not all of them engineers) draw up specifications. Contractual obligations ensure (one hopes) reliability. However, while procurement by the output required rather than a technical specification might encourage the supplier to innovate, it has to be seen in the context of managerial responsibilities. What is the best value for the business?

Acton Works

Acton Works, for many years the central railway overhaul workshops in west London, was opened in 1922. At its maximum extent, the works occupied a 20ha site to the south of Acton Town station and provided facilities for heavy overhaul and reconditioning of all London Transport's railway rolling stock as well as supplying reconditioned wheels and other components to the running depots.

However, overall maintenance requirements were decreasing. Thus underfloor wheel lathes to re-machine the wheels meant that they did not have to be removed from the vehicles first. It was not even necessary to uncouple the vehicles, and a complete four-car set could be drawn progressively across the lathe by winch. Heavy mechanical work was being replaced with increasing requirements for electrical and electronic work.

All car overhauls were transferred to the line depots from 1985, starting with Golders Green. Equipment removed from the vehicles was maintained at a new facility at Acton or by outside contractors.

These main depots have always dealt with day-to-day cleaning, inspection and maintenance. A lifting

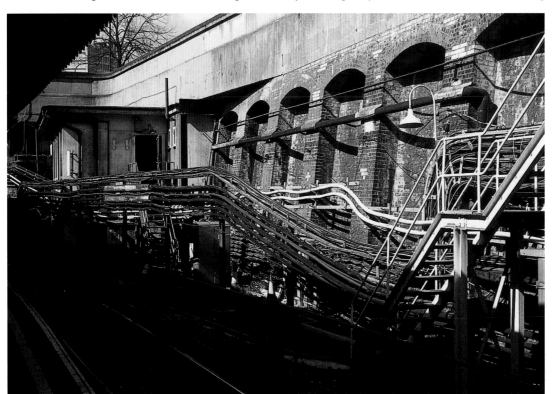

Left: *This tangle of cable is immediately opposite the eastbound passenger platform at Edgware Road (H&C) and was photographed on 9 April 2008. It demonstrates very well how complex the work is of keeping the Underground functioning but also that renewals work cannot be delayed indefinitely.* John Glover

facility and inspection pits both beneath and at the side of the cars were also part of the standard provision, and aided the new tasks. Depot facilities are not always new; Hammersmith remains largely as built by the Great Western Railway on a very restricted site. This does limit the work which can be undertaken there, and the length of train which can be accommodated without dividing it.

Train examination and maintenance

What do the trains need in the way of care? Requirements vary according to the type and the age of the train, but the following is a general guide.

Examination and maintenance is carried out at several levels. On a daily basis, train preparation aims to check that a train is in a safe and proper condition when offered for service, and to ensure that defects reported by operators are acknowledged and corrected. This is essentially a systems check. It covers items such as the tripcock, deadman's handle, door pilot and passenger alarm. The next level up at 14 days is the detailed examination of brake blocks and mechanical parts, the door-operating mechanisms and the current-collecting equipment.

Then there are periodic examinations, which have a fuller agenda. The intention is:
- To ensure trains remain in a wholly serviceable condition
- To examine elements of the train not accessible in normal usage, for damage and degradation

- To check and adjust wearing parts and consumable items to ensure they remain serviceable within defined limits.
- To check secondary protective structural devices.

The intervals between successive car examinations are determined by the rate at which consumables wear out, and the time it is considered prudent to run trains before having a good look underneath. In short, the aim is to make sure that nothing falls off. With consumables, the time between replacements can be increased, but it must be recognised that the rate of wear depends upon the use made of the train. Thus, if a brake block is not fully worn when it is replaced some wastage will result, but this is unavoidable on a time interval rather than usage-based system.

A detailed examination of all equipment is carried out at 30 weeks; more extensive overhaul work is performed at 4 to 4½-year intervals.

Additionally, trains returning to service following maintenance need to be tested. The minimum testing and inspection requirements need to be defined, to ensure the train is fit for service. This is to guard against matters such as the incorrect renewal of wiring, which could induce wrong side failures.

Technical training

One result of the PPP infrastructure contracts was the establishment by Tube Lines of a new centre at Stratford to replace outdated facilities at Acton. Opened in 2005, it comprises sections of varying types

Below: *Long-welded rail is produced at Ruislip and distributed throughout the system with trains hauled by battery locomotives. The end result is far superior to the use of jointed track.*
Gone are the hammer blows caused by the wheels hitting the rail ends, and the damage caused. These are weak points in the track structure, and the fewer of them the better. By its very nature, this is heavy material and of very considerable length. This picture shows some of the storing and loading facilities on 18 May 2004. John Glover

of track, points, signalling equipment and an interlocking machine room, as well as classrooms. Courses offered include track safety and protection, fire training, possessions, and lifts, escalators and machine room safety. There are also a number of signalling courses and train maintenance programmes. There is also an apprenticeship scheme.

The construction of the Tube Lines Skills Training Centre follows directly from the massive infrastructure renewal and investment plans now under way, and the need to ensure that the right skills are available on the Underground at the right time. There are around 250 people attending courses at any one time, and the centre is open 24 hours a day and seven days a week to cater for shift patterns.

Below: *Lots Road power station dates from 1905 and is situated on the north side of the Thames at Chelsea. It was fed by colliery barges, using the adjacent Chelsea Creek. Electricity generation was exclusively for the Underground. This ceased in 2002 and it was decommissioned, but the 'Chelsea monster' is still very much 'there'. It was photographed from the south bank on 22 April 2009.* John Glover

9

LONDON UNDERGROUND LTD

The new strategic planning and management body, London Regional Transport (LRT) was created in June 1984, forming London Underground Ltd (LUL) as a directly controlled transport operation from 1985. LRT also undertook the common activities such as ticketing, marketing and service information.

It represented a complete change of direction and the Docklands Light Railway was hived off, the London Buses subsidiaries were privatised, and other businesses were sold.

In discharging its duties, LRT had to have regard for London's transport needs, and that it needed to break even after grants as required by the Secretary of State for Transport.

The initial emphasis of London Regional Transport was on cost reduction and consolidation, but one of the main factors causing the strategy to be rethought was the upsurge in passenger usage, fuelled by a growing economy and the runaway success of the Travelcard.

Fares policies

The Travelcard defined concentric fares zones around central London. Zone 1 encompassed the Circle line and a little more, with what was later to be termed Zone 6 coinciding more or less with the Greater London boundary. Latterly, Zones 7 to 10 were added for the Underground outside it.

Travelcard tickets were available and priced for the number of zones required, and were valid for unlimited travel on London Underground, London bus services, the Docklands Light Railway, London Tramlink and (later) National Rail services within the zone(s) selected. As season tickets, they were issued for one week or for any period between one month and one year. This gave their holders the freedom to interchange without penalty, and to make additional journeys at no additional cost.

Managing the Underground

In the five years from 1983, unit costs were cut by 15%. Infrastructure investment was more than doubled, both to secure reductions in future running costs and to modernise and improve the amenity value of the system. After years of underfunding, much of the Underground was still squalid, and perceptions of the quality of service offered were correspondingly low.

Neither public nor staff confidence had been improved by the major fire at King's Cross in November 1987 in which 31 persons died, and a sad tale of shortcomings was unravelled by the public inquiry. The railway was not being run professionally, and it ran out of luck. The most lasting result to come out of this incident was a realisation that safety hazards must be identified and rated according to their potential impact and likelihood of happening – and of

Left: The 1959 stock was never operated in anything but unpainted aluminium until London Underground decided to recreate a 'Heritage' train in 1990. This was the result, and the complete train is seen here in Ruislip depot. Two of the DM cars may now be found on the Alderney Railway in the Channel Islands and a DM and a trailer car at Mangapps Farm Railway in Essex. Colour-Rail (LT149)

A one-day off-peak ticket valid from 09:30 gave similar benefits, and this was supplemented by an all-day ticket at a higher price in 2003. Underground single journey fares were also converted to a zonal basis.

In 1991/92, Travelcard sales accounted for 62% of all London Underground revenue. It was hoped that Travelcard would result in a fundamental shift in the market for travel, thus enlarging the core of intensive users whose patronage is critical in sustaining the system.

The fares policies were certainly successful, to the extent that overcrowding and congestion once again became part of the vocabulary of public transport operators in London. Demand was racing ahead, stimulated also by economic growth. Such was the turnaround that the 498 million passenger journeys of 1982 reached 815 million in 1988/89.

the cost of remedial measures. This includes standards, materials, communications and emergency arrangements, and also the need for crowd control plans at major stations and thus the means of providing for the growing problem of congestion relief.

Another result was a complete change of top management.

Travel volumes increase

If poor quality was one problem, the other was growth. Many of the factors affecting the level and pattern of demand for Underground travel are way outside the control of management. Population, employment, personal incomes, car ownership, road conditions and tourism are among those factors. As with personal investment warnings, 'passenger volumes may go down as well as up'. And down they went.

Right: *When the access to the station platforms is gained by steps up from a pedestrian subway beneath the tracks, there are obvious advantages to make it accessible from either side. This is the situation at the Metropolitan's Northwick Park (1923) on 28 June 2008. But how do you make the second side attractive? A well-lit paved footway plus a properly signed entrance helps, and painting all the brickwork white certainly livens up the whole.*
John Glover

But, by 1994/95, volumes had recovered to 764 million and were to continue to rise. They passed the one billion mark for the first time in 2005/06. That, though, is never known in advance, since projections are just that. However, if one is unprepared, the situation can easily become untenable.

It all boiled down to a conclusion that without action being taken, probably irrespective of any fares levels which might be considered reasonable, system capacity was likely to become totally inadequate.

Strategic issues

There were five strategic issues facing London Underground Ltd in the late 1980s:
- The network capacity was constrained at the peak.
- There were service quality as well as safety problems as a result.
- The anticipated growth of demand would be a further 20% at peak and 30% at off-peak by 1997/98.
- Major additions to capacity needed large investments and long lead times.
- LUL had neither the cash nor the borrowing powers to fund extensive new investment in either the short or medium term.

What, then, would be the likely effects of taking various broad courses of action? Four scenarios were painted:

Commercial network. This would make money, and be cash rich within a decade through high fares and the lopping off of the extremities, such as everything north and west of Harrow-on-the-Hill. Lines such as the Bakerloo which are paralleled (in this case mostly by the Jubilee or what were then BR's Watford local services) would close completely. Overall, the network would shrink to about half its present size.

Quality network. The quality of provision would be brought up to predetermined levels, but essentially the system would remain within the limits of the existing infrastructure.

Expanded network. As quality network, but providing additional infrastructure works to relieve congestion and serving new areas of London as could be justified.

London showpiece network. This would be an attempt to make London resemble Paris, but at a capital cost of £10 billion which could come only from outside sources.

Right: *This is a view of the interior of the 1959 stock as refurbished to 'Heritage' specifications. In many ways the treatment afforded to DM 1030 was similar to that for the earlier 1938 stock, but the latter never had strip lighting. The colour scheme was, however, strongly reminiscent.*
John Glover

Left: *The Central Line's fleet of 1992 stock trains are now approaching midlife, having monopolised services on that line for nearly two decades. A train of this stock arrives at the suburban station of East Acton on an eastbound working in April 1995, when it was almost new.* John Glover

Left: *The Epping–Ongar service had the luxury of a passing loop at North Weald, though by now it was disused. A four-car train of 1962 stock is arriving from Epping. It is 22 July 1977, and the slowly diminishing branch service will still be running for another 17 years.* John Glover

Right: The building of a new station at Hillingdon in 1992 was occasioned by the construction of the A40(M) which was to pass beneath the railway. This required the then existing station to be demolished and a new one was built. The road passes beneath the underbridge beyond the platform ends. A train of 1973 Piccadilly Line stock is departing for Cockfosters in March 2003.
John Glover

Right: It is late afternoon at the main entrance to Canary Wharf Jubilee Line station on 22 April 2009, from which multiple escalators descend to the intermediate landing where the ticket office is located. It is then through the ticket barriers and on down via more escalators to platform level. The station was constructed in the former West India Dock, which in a sense makes the surface building of cut-and-cover construction, albeit of a very different era.
John Glover

Performance measures

These were uncomfortable choices, and it was clear that the finances of the business could not be separated from the other factors. A balance needed to be found to take into account financial performance, adequate service quality, volume of service provision and safety. It is simply not tenable to allow more and more passengers to crowd into the system unless it is expanded to cope.

What the customers of London Underground merited was a policy which allowed government funding for major investment in expanding service provision, offset against internal efficiency improvements and restructuring of the business to improve its management, and the results showing within a five-year time scale. There needs to be a co-ordinated framework.

Some of this was within management's ability to deliver, other parts not. Realistically, the returns for private investment in rapid transit are just not there, with the result that public cash is needed in the vast majority of cases.

Making it happen

A total restructuring saw each Underground line made into a profit centre and given its own general manager. These managers were also responsible for costs, revenues, the performance of the physical assets, and of that all-important asset — people. Everything else was a support function. Staff were to be responsible to one named manager.

In the Underground's 1988 'Plan for Action', the company set out a long-term objective that the total service would be of the same standard which is implied by new trains, updated control systems and signalling, well-maintained track and modernised stations. The financial performance needed to be maximised within the constraints of volume and the extension of quality and safety of service. Market potential was to be optimised, and it was essential that long-term total costs were brought down to the lowest possible level.

Central Line

The upgrading proposal for the Central Line was by far the most extensive. The 85 new trains of 1992 stock and their derivation from the 1986 stock have already been discussed. Line refurbishment included the installation of new fixed block signalling and centralised control. The power supply system was replaced and uprated, to allow trains to run faster. There were also minor track realignments to raise speed limits.

Restrictions, such as speeds over the tortuous curves at Bank and the time taken to discharge passengers at Liverpool Street and other busy stations, were as much limits as was the signalling, when it came to increasing service frequency. The whole project was aimed at increasing the total line carrying capacity by about 16%.

In the event, Automatic Train Protection (ATP), which ensures that all traffic moves at a safe speed (and replaces the tripcocks used previously), was introduced to the Central Line by 1997. This was followed by Automatic Train Operation (ATO), which aims to achieve the optimum operational performance in terms of journey time, headway and energy consumption. Antennae on the train pick up the signalling codes which are transmitted through the running rails, and on reaching the target speed, the train drives automatically to that speed. Installation was completed in 2001.

This leads to consistent standards of operation, taking over from the human factor. The running time from West Ruislip to Epping was reduced by 13 minutes.

With ATO centralised control from the new West London Control Centre, the remaining signalboxes along the line were taken out of use progressively.

Northern line

The Northern is the second busiest, with around 850,000 passengers a day. Large-scale investment was needed, and one of the major schemes was Angel station. New office building at Angel had seen traffic more than double in six years. The station was provided only with lifts, and these were replaced by two flights of escalators descending from a new entrance to a circulating area to the west of the previous island platform. The northbound track of this was filled in as was done at Euston when the Victoria Line was built, and a direct passageway made to the new circulating area. A totally new northbound platform was constructed in a new station tunnel, and the line diverted into it. Work was completed in 1992.

A number of shorter-term improvements were also undertaken. Transfer of additional trains from the Bakerloo as part of the repercussions of the delivery of the 1983 tube stock boosted the number in service. Highgate depot was reopened and modernised, while 11 stations at the southern end of the line were refurbished. The dot-matrix information displays were upgraded, with more passenger security measures at the southern end. Dot-matrix indicators were provided in some ticket halls so that passengers need descend to platform level only when their train's arrival is imminent. Aerials were installed in the ceilings of underground passages so that staff could remain in contact by personal radio.

Left: *At Finchley Road the Jubilee Line comes to the surface through portals once used by the Metropolitan Railway. This is 19 km and 14 stations from Canning Town, where it originally went underground.*
On 29 April 2009, a train of 1996 stock enters the northbound platform. Cross-platform interchange to the Metropolitan is available here, and many passengers prefer to use this rather than the escalators and stairs which are necessary if changing between the two lines at Baker Street.
John Glover

Right: *The 1983 stock for the Jubilee line was not a great success; its single doors in particular were a limitation on the rates of passenger loading and unloading at stations. In July 1989, a train of this stock descends the bank from the flyover which takes this, the Metropolitan and the Chiltern Railways route over the North London Line. It may be noted that the points for the turnback siding in the centre are set in a central position. This ensures that a runaway stood in the siding would be derailed harmlessly, and not obstruct either the northbound (left) or southbound Jubilee line (right), and on which the train is travelling.*
John Glover

Right: *Tucked under the arches at the side of a railway bridge over a main road is not perhaps an ideal station entrance, but this is what has been done with Kilburn, Jubilee line. The projecting canopy and the hanging sign make it clear what the premises offer on 26 June 2008.*
John Glover

Rolling stock

At that time, the Northern was operated by a mixture of 1959–62 and 1972 Mk I stock trains, very much the bits and pieces which were left over from other lines, and they needed replacement. The Northern has long continuous tunnel gradients to the north, and a high proportion is in tunnel. Station platforms are also relatively restricted in length, and operationally it would be desirable to get away from an inflexible seven-car formation. It was announced late in 1994 that a new fleet of 106 trains (the 1995 stock) was to be built by Metro-Cammell (later part of GEC-Alsthom) in an entirely new form of contract.

Meanwhile, refurbishment was carried out on three trains of 1972 stock as the remainder were too old to justify it. The new décor was designed to offer a brash exterior and a homely interior. Lighting was softened to reduce glare, while providing the much-liked end bulkhead lights to brighten up the gloomy corners. Repositioned grab rails encouraged standing passengers to move away from the door area. Panels and fittings assessed as potential fire hazards were replaced, and public address fitted. Comparable work was carried out on the very similar Victoria (1967) and Bakerloo (1972 Mk II) stock.

Unfortunately, the arrival of the new trains was not matched with the strengthening of power supplies and

the renewal of signalling. In prospect was a reduction of journey times, for which the permanent way needed to be brought up to scratch, coupled with increased service frequencies. Flat-bottomed long-welded rail would become standard equipment.

These would have to wait for the Public Private Partnerships, which were still a few years away.

Signalling

The Northern's capacity had been reduced in the years of passenger losses by signalling-simplification schemes. Transmission-based signalling is the means to overcome the problem, through which the train service might be increased to 32tph south of Kennington and 24tph on all branches north of there. Journey times via the City are four minutes longer than via Charing Cross. This though could be a recipe for conflict and hence delays.

With the new signalling, the 106-train fleet signals its position and speed via the track to a central computer, which then analyses the information every 0.5sec and 'instructs' the train accordingly. Such measures have taken precedence over earlier ideas such as splitting the line into two parts, as already discussed.

However, terminating all Charing Cross trains at Kennington by sending them round the loop may yet be found necessary, and also making the services to each of the Edgware/High Barnet branches more selective.

The new ATO signalling (Transmission Based Train Control) for the Northern Line will be in place by the end of 2011 and the new Highgate Control Centre replaces the Coburg Street facility.

Line capacity

The capacity of lines is governed primarily by train lengths and service frequencies. More trains and longer trains were one of the options being pursued by British Rail, but on the existing Underground with traditional signalling, it was considered that something like 30 trains per hour is the realistic maximum. This is despite schedules on the Bakerloo and District lines in the past offering a (perhaps theoretical) 34 or 36tph. Train capacities vary, but using the Underground's formal loading standards, an 8xA-stock formation will carry 680, while both 6xC-stock and most tube stock trains will carry 550. More passengers can of course squeeze themselves on.

New objectives

In the spring of 1989, London Regional Transport were set new objectives for their rail services by the government. These were:

- To carry through the recommendations arising from the King's Cross fire
- To provide for the continuing increase in traffic on the Underground, and for growing needs in Docklands.
- To improve the quality of services and security for the traveller.

With the scene having changed significantly, formal targets were set for service quality. Among these was the performance of lifts and escalators. Only 75% were in working order in 1989, which was freely admitted to be unacceptable. Those on the Victoria Line, which were only 20 years old, were failing. Underground escalators may now have been the cleanest in the world in the aftermath of King's Cross, but the incapacity of the industry and the high loads being carried for hours at a time played havoc with performance. New escalators were being installed at 12 a year for the foreseeable future.

Right: *The construction of a further two tracks from Barking to Upminster was undertaken by the LMS as the successors to the Tilbury company, and these were opened in 1932. Becontree was one of them, seen here from the road outside. As with many of the stations on this line, access is from a road bridge spanning the railway. The architecture is functional, and most are very similar. The picture was taken on 10 April 2008.* John Glover

Below left: *Roding Valley has street entrances from both platforms, which are connected by overbridge. As can be seen there are no barriers (this is the westbound side). At lightly used stations such as this, there is a need to provide access for all and to keep staffing costs to a minimum.* John Glover

Far right: *The guard was the company ambassador, ready to dispense helpful words of advice to inquiring passengers, though it must be said that some were more adept at this than others. This scene is at King's Cross St Pancras on the Northern line. The last day of Underground guards was on 27 January 2000; it was also the final appearance of the 1959 stock in passenger service.* John Glover

In escalators, as in so much else, the largely unsung role of the engineer is crucial. Here too there are changes. Technology offers the ability to squeeze more out of existing infrastructure, to increase construction benefits and to reduce operating costs. But new technology is demanding. New skills are needed, a control over specifications is essential, while there us a need to learn from those outside. It is much more cost effective to learn from the mistakes of others!

Fares revenue

The Underground needed more revenue. By the end of the 1980s, it was noticeable that official noises were beginning to be made about fares levels; a slow increase in real fares since LRT took over in 1984 was approaching a cumulative 20% five years later. The harder line asserted that fares had not grown faster than earnings, and that fares levels still offered good value for money. The users of the system are predominantly under 35 years old, while 70% are in the ABC1 social groups and relatively well off. With a government view that passengers must pay for the benefits they receive, further real fares increases seemed inevitable. However, pricing limitations by the Rail Regulator on National Railways' fares also affect London Underground pricing.

Such, at any rate, was the view of the Monopolies and Mergers Commission (MMC) in their 1991 report. With economic recession biting into traffic levels, and following some financial misjudgements, the Company had to make economies. The MMC were critical of the physically decayed state of much of the infrastructure. 'The public's perception of an erratic, overcrowded and poorly maintained service in many areas is broadly correct,' they said, albeit acknowledging that the overall picture was more favourable. They too concluded that higher fares would be needed in order to finance investment and renewals, endorsing as they did the need to inject £¾ million a year for the foreseeable future.

Insufficient investment leads to higher asset age and failure rate, to higher maintenance costs and the costs of inspections and repairs. This then results in a reduction of funds available for investment and thus to even higher asset age and failure rates … and so on.

Investment programme, or not?

Yet, it was not to be, for in their autumn 1992 statement the government cut the promised 1993/94 investment programme by a third, with similar reductions in subsequent years. The result was a drastic slowing down or cancellation of projects, with station refurbishment being the worst hit area. Station modernisations, like those carried out successfully at Edgware Road (Bakerloo), Gloucester Road, Hammersmith (District and Piccadilly), and Hillingdon were among the schemes most easily dispensed with. Track reconditioning plus attention to tunnels, earthworks, bridges, power supplies, pumps, drainage and ventilation, lifts and escalators, and lighting are, perhaps regrettably but certainly realistically, far more important.

London Underground returned to the fray in 1993, when the 'Decently Modern Metro' was launched. Its aim is to provide up-to-date infrastructure supporting a railway which is safe, quick, reliable, clean,

Left: *Two bay platforms were provided at Stratford in the reconstructed station for the electrified shuttle service to Fenchurch Street, which never materialised. One was adapted for use by the Docklands Light Railway, though it is no longer used. The other, Platform 7, seen here with no track, could have provided same-level interchange to the westbound Central Line (also seen here) and the local Shenfield services. This view was taken in March 2002. John Glover*

Right: *The refurbishment of the C stock trains replaced blocks of four (2x2) transverse seats with the equivalent longitudinal seating, as shown here in August 1997. That way, the amount of standing space available was increased considerably, with no seat loss. This would seem to be the generalised layout of the future for Underground operations (and for London Overground too). How suitable it is for the longer distance journeys which some will be making is perhaps another matter.* John Glover

comfortable and efficient, and which gives good value for money. Was this too much for Londoners to expect, with a total spend of about £7.5 billion over a decade?

Of this, London Underground themselves might fund a quarter out of revenue gains and cost reduction; the remainder would have to come from the government. This turned out to be rather more than the government was intending to spend! Nevertheless, London Underground was setting itself a goal to become financially self-sufficient, once the investment backlog was cleared.

Railways Act 1993

One indirect consequence of the Railways Act 1993 was the transfer of three parts of the railway system in the London area to the Underground. This took place on 1 April 1994, when London Underground became the owner and operator of the Waterloo & City, the Wimbledon branch of the District beyond Putney Bridge station, albeit excluding Wimbledon station itself, and the Kensington (Olympia) stub end.

The Underground-owned network increased in length by about 8km. Acquisition included the liabilities as well as the benefits; thus Fulham Bridge (the railway bridge over the Thames at Putney) needed £7 million worth of repairs after being struck by a barge in 1991. Power supplies and signalling remained with what is now Network Rail. Also new to the Underground was the inheritance of the two Travelators installed at Bank W&C station.

Perhaps a more far-reaching change was the need for the Underground to develop a safety case under the Railway (Safety Case) Regulations, 1994. This demonstrates the organisation's ability to conduct its operations safely, with the principle that the Railway

Infrastructure Controller has overall responsibility for safe railway operation over that infrastructure. In the case of London Underground, this needed to cover the three aspects of stations, trains and infrastructure. LUL had to satisfy Her Majesty's Railway Inspectorate on this, but also as an operator had to have its own case accepted by Railtrack where it ran trains over Railtrack lines to Harrow & Wealdstone and Richmond. It also had to accept cases from other operators running on LUL lines, notably between Harrow-on-the-Hill and Amersham. This included freight operations.

Aldwych and Ongar

By the 1990s, two short sections of the system were deemed to have outlived their usefulness. An Underground line closure is a rare event, yet on 30 September 1994 both the Holborn-Aldwych (Piccadilly) and the Epping–Ongar (Central) branches saw their last trains.

At Aldwych, daily usage by 450 passengers was judged insufficient to justify spending around £3 million on replacing the 1906 lifts.

For Ongar and the intermediate branch station of North Weald, a residual traffic of 80 passengers/day over a single line with deteriorating track was clearly not enough.

These were not the sort of traffic volumes for which the Underground was best suited.

London Regional Passengers Committee

When the 1984 Act took effect, consumer representation on matters to do with London Underground became the responsibility of the London Regional Passengers Committee (LRPC). The Committee was the official but independent voice of the public transport users, and acted as a focus for passengers' views. In law, the LRPC had certain duties, a few rights, but no powers.

The LRPC's aims included the promotion and development of an integrated public transport network, and to represent the interests of all passengers to operators and any other parties involved. Penalty fares were introduced by London Underground in 1994, which was backed up by an unambiguous policy of paying before travel or face the penalty. From the point of view of LRPC, this measure, however justified, was largely responsible for a huge increase in consumer complaints.

Jubilee Line

A Parliamentary Bill was deposited in 1989 for the 16km Jubilee Line extension (JLE) to Stratford. This followed pledges of financial support from private-sector developers in Docklands, though these turned out to be only 15% or so of the anticipated capital costs. The chosen alignment did not even appear on the list of options in the Central London Rail Study, but was the subject of the later East London Rail Study.

The scheme was authorised on 29 October 1993 by the Secretary of State for Transport, and the LRT Chairman Sir Wilfred Newton promised completion by 29 March 1998 and to budget. Both promises were sadly astray; opening of the whole line, in stages, was just achieved by the end of 1999, while the final cost was almost twice the £1.9bn anticipated.

Traffic expectations

Expectations for the Jubilee line extension were set out in detail when the authorising Bill was before parliament. As anticipated, the busiest section is eastbound in the morning peak.

Thus a flow of 20,500 passengers per hour on leaving Baker Street would fall to a low of 14,400 from Westminster to Waterloo, on leaving which they would rise to 17,000, and again to 18,400 on leaving London Bridge. This reflected the influx of between four and five thousand commuters from the main-line railways at each of these stations. However, numbers fall abruptly with 14,700 alighting at Canary Wharf, with only 3,500 on trains leaving that point, and remaining at broadly that level through to the Jubilee Line terminus at Stratford.

Similar effects were noticeable in the westbound direction with 6,000 or so passengers joining at both Stratford and West Ham. Only 7,200 of the 17,600 then expected to be on board alight at Canary Wharf. Others travel on, mostly to the West End, being joined by more commuters from the main lines at London Bridge, Southwark (for Waterloo East) and Waterloo. A decade after the line opened in 1999, Canary Wharf in fare Zone 2 is the only one of the 10 busiest Underground stations which is located outside the central-area Zone 1. It is ranked seventh, and was used by 44 million passengers in 2008. That is 80% above the 24 million recorded five years earlier in 2003.

This capacious station is of cut-and-cover

Below: The Victoria Line look-alikes for the Northern were restricted to 30 trains built by Metro-Cammell. They were designed for crew operation. A train of the 1972 Mk I stock is seen here leaving Morden depot to enter service on 7 May 1990. These trains were eventually to be disbanded with some vehicles finding their way to strengthen the Bakerloo and Victoria fleets. John Glover

Above: *The 1992 stock consists of a total of 680 vehicles for the Central Line, or 700 if the Waterloo & City is included. In May 2001 a train arrives at Chigwell with its wide and open platforms from the Hainault direction. The branch is no longer operated as a shuttle service from Woodford; all trains run to and from far-off places such as West Ruislip.*
John Glover

construction in a box structure 280m long, 35m wide at the lower levels and 27m high. The length is dictated by the need to accommodate a 130m long platform and a scissors crossover at the lowest level. There is an intermediate ticket hall level reached by escalators at 10m above platform level, and this is 180m long and 10.8m high. Further escalators take passengers to ground level. There are a total of 20 escalators and three lifts, but there are only two platforms.

Construction

Civil works covering the tunnels and station construction was divided unto 12 geographically-based contracts. These covered the tunnel boring and station construction. To these were added separate contracts for trackwork procurement, the rolling-stock depot, and the service control centre at Neasden.

Electrical and mechanical design and construct contracts covered ventilation, both at stations and in tunnels, services generally, works locomotives and rolling stock, electrical items such as power cables, conductor rail and power intake at West Ham substation, depot equipment, communications, signalling systems and control, lifts and escalators, passenger rolling stock, platform-edge doors for the underground section and the Underground ticketing system.

The extension is entirely underground for the first 12.4km of construction; rising the ground level just south of Canning Town, it is a further 3.6km to the Stratford terminus. The line passes beneath the

Thames four times, between Westminster and Waterloo, between Canada Water and Canary Wharf, between Canary Wharf and North Greenwich, and again between North Greenwich and Canning Town. It thus gives multiple opportunities for cross-river journeys and also makes them simple to achieve.

Underground construction south of the Thames is not simple, with London clay giving way to sands and gravels. The latter are frequently waterlogged. The work was carried out under compressed air conditions, with water forced back into the excavated ground while the tunnel segments were put in place. The tunnels return to London clay at North Greenwich There are 11 stations on the extension, and all but two (Bermondsey and North Greenwich) provide interchange with other lines. The result is that every other Underground station can be reached with one change of train only, though a second change can sometimes be advisable. The one exception is Kensington Olympia.

The line control centre is at Neasden, with rolling-stock depots here and at Stratford Market on the west side of the formation.

New standards

The extension was built to rather higher standards than those used hitherto; on the underground section, the new running tunnels were bored to 4.35m diameter, to allow for the installation of a side walkway. This aids maintenance and considerably eases the detraining of passengers should this be necessary. It does not, however, allow for larger-diameter rolling stock, since the existing tunnels north from Green Park were constructed to 3.7m diameter as was previous practice. The platform tunnel diameters are 7.7m with a platform length of 130m.

A typical station layout underground includes a ventilation shaft at each end, emergency stairs and a lift for disabled passengers. The lifts can also be used by those accompanied by children or with luggage. Escalators are in groups of three or four, with either one or two banks needed to cover the vertical distances. Thus, a remarkable total of 115 escalators have been provided on the extension as a whole, representing very nearly half as many again as existed previously on the whole of London Underground.

Station control rooms were provided, equipped with an information management system to enable the whole operation of the station and associated equipment to be monitored and controlled.

On the edges of the platforms, automatic platform doors are installed for the first time in Britain on a commercial railway, as opposed to people-mover installations as may be found at Gatwick Airport.

Platform screen doors

The electrically-operated platform doors separate the passenger from the train, and double or single doors are installed to coincide with the position of those on the train. As it arrives, the accurate positioning of the train by the driver is critical to the success of the doors; too far away, and neither the train doors nor the platform doors will open. The two are synchronised to work together. Potentially, there can be severe effects on station dwell time; besides the lengthening of train journey times, this is also a major determinant of line capacity.

The installation of platform doors promotes the smooth running of the whole ventilation system, controlling wind direction, velocity and hence platform draughts caused by the movement of the trains. They also reduce the circulation of accumulated dirt. Doors also keep passengers safe from trains, deter suicides and prevent the throwing of rubbish onto the track.

On the debit side, each door needs its own operating system, with sensors to detect any obstruction from a passenger to the handle of a bag. The net result is a doubling up of the train door mechanisms and safety devices, so there are roundly twice as many things to go wrong.

While the installation of platform doors is achievable with new construction, it is much more difficult to retro-fit them to existing lines, or stations from Green Park northwards on the Jubilee. Effectively, they take up part of the platform depth as measured from the back wall, and this is already less than desirable in many cases. More perplexing is the problem of severely curved platforms; while straight platforms have always been desirable to minimise the train-to-platform gap at all points, and to offer a clear view for staff (or cameras) along the length of the train, there are many places featuring curves, or even reverse curves, for a number of historic reasons. Both problems could be addressed, but they do imply major disruption and expense in order to achieve universal provision at below-ground stations.

Left: *The acquisition of the Waterloo & City Line by London Underground from British Rail in 1994 came with a nearly new set of rolling stock. These were in Network SouthEast livery until major refurbishment took place many years later. This is unit No 482.507 having recently arrived at Bank from Waterloo on 11 July 1994.* John Glover

LONDON UNDERGROUND LIMITED

Installation at above-ground locations would have to take into account the effects of exposure of the doors and their mechanisms to high winds, hot sunshine, rain and snow, unless the station itself was largely covered over.

Rolling stock

New trains were required also for the Jubilee, and the decision was made to replace the 1983 stock trains (of which there were only 31 anyway, divided into two batches) and build afresh. This avoided all the compatibility problems and mixtures of stock.

Key aspects of the extension

Some of the findings have been as follows:
- Westminster station is almost as important as Bank for connections.
- Southwark has low population density but had special justification as an area needing stimulus. It also offered an interchange alternative to for National Rail passengers using Charing Cross.
- London Bridge is important for West End and central area distribution, and also Tate Bankside.
- Bermondsey is a high-density area with social problems, and the Underground provides access to jobs.
- Canada Water interchange takes 20 secs.

- Canary Wharf station is not as well sited as the DLR station, as there was too much development already in place. That subjects many to a wet and windy walk, though it can be accomplished under cover. Canary Wharf has become a centre of office employment to rival both the City and the West End.
- At Stratford, 70% of ticket issues are for Underground destinations rather than National Rail.

Millennium celebrations

The Jubilee extension opened in time for the Millennium celebrations, both at The Dome at North Greenwich and in central London. It was decided to run Underground services all night long in the 42-hour period from the start of traffic on Friday 31 December 1999 to last trains on Saturday 1 January 2000. It was anticipated that 2½ million passengers would be carried over this extended opening period.

This required special attention to the likely number of visitors and when they would be travelling, how to deal with those who were intoxicated, crowd control arrangements, station dwell times, selective station closures, the provision of engineering support but with scheduled maintenance suspended, use of the communication systems, and staff authority to enter police-cordoned areas.

Above: *Acton Town is a busy junction, as well as the location for Ealing Common depot. From the station overbridge, two trains of Piccadilly Line 1973 stock can be seen. One is approaching from Heathrow with a Cockfosters service, the other is in the turnback siding. At the top of the picture, six D stock trains seem to be peering over the parapet like a group of old ladies, trying to check on what is happening below.* John Glover

The entire operation was completed with no incidents of any significance, to the great credit of London Underground management and staff alike. A similar exercise was mounted for the Queen's Golden Jubilee on the night of 3/4 June 2002.

Project execution

The verdict on the management of the Jubilee Line extension work came later in 2000, in a report commissioned by the government from Ove Arup. 'The JLE was delayed and its cost massively inflated because of LUL's lack of strong management and expertise. 'There was a failure to appoint lead contractors, an absence of incentives, constant design changes and attempts to use complex untried technology.'

This last was a reference to the provision of advanced ATP signalling, for which conventional signalling was substituted in the rush to get the project up and running in time for the millennium. This could accommodate a maximum of 24 trains per hour.

The report criticised LUL's decision to use in-house managers and the lack of a realistic initial risk assessment. According to LUL, the final cost was £3.5 bn.

There was also the small matter of a claim from the Canary Wharf group over the failure to provide the specified service levels as a result of the signalling problems. The company had promised £500m over 24 years towards the capital costs, but on the expectation that service frequencies would be higher.

Jubilee developments

The Christmas/New Year period of 2005/06 was used to install the seventh car in the then fleet and to introduce four new trains. Operation of a mixed fleet during a changeover was considered, but rejected. Thus 59x6-cars became 63x7-cars, with the addition of 87 new vehicles.

Maintenance is contracted by Tube Lines to Alstom and is undertaken at Stratford Market, with cleaning etc at Stanmore. Neasden is used for stabling.

The installation of Automatic Train Operation moving block Seltrac signalling from Thales was completed in 2010, rather later than intended, and a similar system is being installed on the Northern Line. This allows more trains to be operated, with computer controlled and thus uniform braking and acceleration rates. The capacity increase is around one third, but it also concentrate wear on particular sections of track. This in turn requires more use of the depot wheel lathe and new maintenance schedules.

The line is now controlled entirely from Neasden, the Baker Street control room having been closed.

The new third platform at Stanmore, to ease turnround arrangements, was commissioned at the end of 2009.

Below: *A train of 1972 Mk II stock leaves Wembley Park for Charing Cross at the then southern end of the Jubilee Line. It sports the unusual red-doors livery which only this stock carried. The fleet was later transferred to the Bakerloo where it monopolises all services, with the help of some transferred-in 1972 Mk I vehicles.* John Glover

10

TRANSPORT FOR LONDON

Since the abolition of the Greater London Council in 1986, there had been no democratically elected city-wide authority. The new plan was for a Greater London Authority (GLA), with a Mayor and Assembly which would be directly elected. The GLA was to have strategic functions, one of which was transport, and the 1997 consultation paper proposed a new body to assume the functions of London Transport and much else besides. This was in the fulfilment of the Labour government's election manifesto.

Greater London Authority Act, 1999

The Greater London Authority Act 1999 was the means of returning public transport in London to municipal control. Under it, the Mayor of London, acting on behalf of the Authority, develops and implements policies for the promotion and encouragement of a safe, integrated, efficient and economic transport service to, from and within Greater London. The Authority sets fares and service levels for all services provided by its executive body Transport for London (TfL), and may give instructions and guidance in relation to the provision of rail services in Greater London (with some limitations.

The mayor has to produce an Integrated Transport Strategy, which must be consistent with the

Underground investment

One of the largest problems facing the Underground has been obtaining the funds needed to maintain and update the infrastructure. As this book has demonstrated, the Underground is old, diverse and difficult to manage. The assets needed to be got into order, with safety requirements met.

Care of the infrastructure had not ranked highly in political priorities over the years; as long as nothing falls apart, there is little incentive to spend money on largely unseen assets. Votes are not won by cleaning out drainage systems and providing new pumps to empty them. However, what you do get is declining service levels, while operating costs rise.

Yet some quite major things were going wrong, and

Left: The entrance to High Barnet station is on a steep pedestrian slope, which gives access to the ticket office area and then straight onto the upper level of the footbridge spanning all three platforms. This is a very convenient, albeit slightly unconventional arrangement. This photograph of 1 June 2009 shows the works under way to provide full disabled access. A second barrier line is being introduced adjacent to the original station building on Platform 1, which is fine for trains departing from or arriving at that platform. Other users will have to pass beyond the end of the terminal tracks shown here to reach the island Platform, nos 2 and 3. Each barrier line will have to be staffed. John Glover

government's national transport policies. This strategy forms the framework for projects promoted by the Authority.

The first mayoral election was on 4 May 2000. Ken Livingstone took office and Transport for London was established on 3 July 2000. TfL is responsible specifically for public transport, the network of roads, working with boroughs, and planning across all modes. On the public transport side, TfL was structured into five divisions representing buses, Underground, Victoria Coach Station, Docklands Light Railway and London River Services. The Secretary of State was given powers to dissolve London Regional Transport.

The remit of the consumer group LRPC was revised, and it is now the London Transport Users Committee (LTUC) or London Travelwatch.

the partial failure of power supplies on a number of occasions had led to prolonged stoppages of trains. Eventually, this was dealt with under a Private Finance Initiative scheme, and the power for traction is now completely outsourced. There are a number of other examples, too. Private funds provide the investment needed and deliver the goods, with the company paying a usage charge.

Apart from government funding usually being too low to achieve what was needed, there were other problems. In recent times, the Central Line had starved the rest of network of investment, with the result that LU lost confidence. (Funds for the Jubilee Line extension project were ring-fenced). Another was the annuality of the process; this year may be all right, but how much do we get next year, and the year after that?

Right: *This view of Goodge Street Northern Line station entrance on 1 June 2009 shows the extensive reconstruction works then under way at street level. Such scenes are commonplace on the Underground system and are yet another indication of the extent of the renewals in progress.* John Glover

Right: *This mid-morning view of the eastbound platform at East Putney on 1 June 2009 shows a good number of passengers waiting for their next service. Urban rail services thrive on volume; movement of people is their purpose. The extension of the Underground into low-density housing areas as typically represented by (say) fares zones 5 and above, although much appreciated, is not what true Metro operation is really about. East Putney is on the Zone 2/3 boundary.* John Glover

Money on infrastructure work cannot be spent at short notice, and Underground funding was always in competition with other deserving causes such as the National Health Service.

PPP possibilities

The PPP concept is based on the public sector working in partnership with the private sector to improve quality and effectiveness of public services. This is done through the provision of capital assets and output-based services, which seek to provide better value than the traditional method of asset acquisition. It encourages:

- A long-term partnership between LUL and private sector companies.
- The intensive programming of work on a scale never previously undertaken on London Underground
- The delivery of new projects in the order that gives the most benefits to costs and long-term whole-life benefits.

The PPP is about enabling LUL to deliver a series of objectives. The key challenges were identified as asset health, which was in long-term decline and needing a sizeable injection of funds, and service performance. In the long term this was to meet growing passenger demand, but short-term performance was not good enough and needed to improve. Value for money was always an important criterion; this would depend on the risks incurred and who shouldered them, but also on the flexibility and enforceability of the 30-year contracts. There was also the safety risk, which must be as low as reasonably practicable (ALARP).

Fundamental aspects of the PPP are that:

- Financial risk is transferred from the public to the private sector.
- The public sector specifies the output required, but not how it is to be done.
- It creates incentives for the private sector to keep costs down.
- Delivery within the specified parameters and quality standards are matters for the private sector to achieve.
- The private sector is remunerated by performance-related charges made for the use of those assets.

Disagreement

Could the PPP approach be used for the much larger and more diverse areas of the infrastructure generally, and the trains? The government thought so, but the mayor disagreed. The upshot was that, as set up, Transport for London was not given responsibility for London Underground. LUL remained a limited company with its headquarters in 55 Broadway, whereas TfL was located in Victoria Street. The government decided that London Underground would only be transferred to the control of the mayor when the Public Private Partnership (PPP) deals for the maintenance of the infrastructure had been completed. This proved to be a much longer task than expected. The prolonged and at times acrimonious wrangling between the mayor and the government meant that years, rather than months, passed with the matter unresolved.

The size of the Underground and hence the tasks must not be underestimated. There is now a total of 402km of route with 270 stations, on which 526 peak hour trains run and 3¼ million passenger journeys a day are made. It is a huge enterprise, and London is very dependent upon it.

In retrospect, it was perhaps unfortunate that the alternatives considered in 1996 were not discussed openly. These were:

- No change, whatever the present faults.
- Selling off the Underground as a single unit, with a share or a bond issue.
- A horizontal split as in the National Railways privatisation, or
- A vertically integrated structure with groups of lines each sold off separately.

The PPP method adopted meant that London Underground remains in the public sector, although it is fair to ask whether it really matters as to who owns the organisation. The Underground passed to Transport for London on 15 July 2003, but only after all the PPP contracts were signed.

Below: The cleaning up of Earl's Court District Line station has brought more light to the platforms, seen here on 22 April 2009 from the new bridge built to provide lift access from street level to the two islands. Here, a D stock train to Richmond approaches, while on the left is a C stock train from Wimbledon to Edgware Road. The ancient platform indicators have been refurbished and reinstated. John Glover

Implementation

Three infrastructure companies (Infracos) were formed within London Underground; shadow running started in September 1999, and they became wholly owned subsidiary companies in April 2000.

The companies were formed as follows:

Infraco BCV   Bakerloo, Central, Victoria lines
Infraco JNP   Jubilee, Northern, Piccadilly lines
Infraco SSL   all subsurface lines

It will be noted that Infraco BCV was made up of the three lines that serve Oxford Circus, while the apparent omission of the Waterloo & City Line is covered by the remark that 'when you shake the Central Line packet, you get the Waterloo & City as a free gift'. What it is to be a London Underground spokesman!

While all Infracos incorporate a range of skills and consultancy services, physical assets are not split so easily. As set up, BCV included the Train Modification Unit (refurbishment, repair), TrackForce (specialised maintenance, renewal and reconditioning) and Track Workshops (long welded rail, point and crossings). Infraco JNP included the specialist activities of Transplant (railway engineering support vehicles and equipment), Distribution Services (specialised road vehicles and those customised for railway usage, haulage and waste management services), and the Emergency Response Unit. Infraco SSL had Railway Engineering Workshops (overhauls of anything from traction motors to signals to clocks). These are activities which were carried out on behalf of all Infracos.

The final agreements for Infraco JNP were signed on 31 December 2002 by Tube Lines, a consortium of Bechtel, Amey and Jarvis. Both Infraco BCV and Infraco SSL went to Metronet on 14 May 2003.

The Agreements

The PPP Agreements set out a performance-related incentive and penalty scheme to remunerate the Infracos for the improvements they make to the network. There are four individual measures:

Availability. The aggregate number of hours lost to customers that are the Infraco's responsibility, such as signal failure. A more reliable service means fewer lost customer hours.

Journey Times Capability. A performance measure looking at the capability and capacity of the system to move large numbers of passengers through it quickly. Mainly influenced by line upgrades and rolling stock performance.

Service Points. A measurement of the response time to faults on the system, and how quickly they are repaired. Better performance is demonstrated by fewer points.

Ambience. The customer environment, including information and the general condition of stations and trains measured in points, the more the better.

The Infracos develop a work plan which balances the maintenance and investment needed to reach the performance targets set, but London Underground specify a number of improvements which must be made by a given date. These include station refurbishment, replacement of train fleets and track replacement.

Tube Lines

The following is a summary of Tube Lines' plans. Over the 30-year contract, Tube Lines will:

- Upgrade the signalling on all three lines (Jubilee, Northern, Piccadilly), bringing increases in capacity and reliability, and reducing journey times.
- The Jubilee upgrade will be completed in 2009 (though this was not actually achieved).
- The Northern upgrade will be completed in 2011.
- The Piccadilly upgrade will be completed in 2014.
- Upgrade all Tube Lines' 100 stations with an emphasis on improving security, information and the general environment for passengers. 97 will be upgraded by 2010.
- Introduce a new fleet of trains on the Piccadilly line in 2014 and refurbish the fleet on the other two lines.
- Replace and refurbish 320km of track, 79 lifts and 227 escalators.
- Improve the general travelling environment for passengers.
In the first 7½-year period, Tube Lines planned to spend over £4.5bn.

Payment

Infracos are paid monthly by the Infrastructure Service Charge, the level of which varies according to performance on each of the measure set.

There is provision for a Periodic Review of the contractual obligations and remuneration every 7 years of the Agreement, which runs for 30 years in total. These reviews are conducted by the independent PPP Arbiter and the first of these is due for implementation in 2010. The prices are not fixed beyond the first renewal point.

When the Agreement comes to and end, the assets must be returned in a satisfactory state of health.

Thus the infrastructure companies provide the necessary 'capability' and London Underground provides predetermined levels of access to the track for maintenance and renewals, eg the times at which the current will be switched off and then back on again. Longer periods of work are dealt with as 'minor closures'. Infracos have 'points' to spend on these, while there is some flexibility for London Underground.

Programme

The programme saw £10.5bn invested in the system over the subsequent 15 years, with a further £6.5bn on maintenance. The concentration on results means that a requirement to raise capacity, as on the Victoria Line,

Above: *Work on track replacement at Colindale is seen well under way in this view from the south of the station and looking towards London. The central track is a siding which is used to reverse trains here; that being dug out is the south-bound. Means have to be found of getting all the equipment to site, and the station is of little help in that respect. The bus outside may be on rail replacement duties, but is more likely to be an ordinary service vehicle. There is a lot to be done before normal services can be restored.*
Author's collection

meant a step up in capability. This does not, in itself, require a fleet of new trains, though these are now being provided. New trains are the most expensive part of a line upgrade. Renewal of the signalling is equally important, as well as track condition, etc.

Not all work forms part of the PPP contracts. Thus London Underground remained in the lead with the securing of powers under the Transport & Works Act procedures, and also with line extensions. This was also the case with major station capacity works, plus legislative and other mandatory changes such as safety. On these issues, risk transfer was not practicable.

Metronet

The two Metronet contracts for the Sub-Surface Lines (SSL) and the Bakerloo, Central and Victoria lines (BCV) had similar provisions, but regrettably the company incurred huge cost over-runs. Metronet was criticised in an Extraordinary Review by the PPP Arbiter in November 2006 for not performing in an economic or efficient manner, and went into administration on 18 July 2007.

According to the National Audit Office, the main cause was that Metronet contracted to use its shareholders and their contractors as suppliers, rather than go through the process of competitive tendering. The executive management of Metronet changed frequently and was unable to manage the work of its supply chain. The loss to the taxpayer was put at between £170m and £410m.

In May 2008, Metronet came out of administration and was transferred to Transport for London, with assets and staff then to London Underground in December 2008.

Line upgrades

'Transforming the Tube' is TfL parlance for the substantial line upgrade programme. This lasts until 2022, and by then the Underground will have 30% extra capacity overall compared with that offered at peak in 2006. This includes the use of new trains (with regenerative braking) and signalling systems, as well as the other major works being undertaken such as track replacement, station reconstructions, ventilation improvements, new control centres and communication systems, and power upgrades. Service reliability, frequencies and the capacity offered will all benefit.

The impact will be different on each line, and some details of some of the major schemes will be found in these pages. This will not and cannot be the end of such works, but they will mark a very considerable achievement for a system which was increasingly showing its age in an era of relentless increases in its usage.

Investment programme

The investment programme requires large sums, and perhaps of interest are the proportions required in the different areas of expenditure. The following refers to that for the period 2005–10:

Stations   30%
Signalling   17%
Rolling stock   11%
Track   11%
Interchange   8%
Communications 6%
Structures   6%
Power supplies 6%
Other   5%

The importance of the station works is immediately apparent, and it is notable that signalling ranks above both rolling stock and track. Track though is the foundation of the railway, and well-maintained track is essential to deliver a safe and reliable service.

Terrorist action

There are always unconnected events to divert the attention. On Thursday 7 July 2005, three bombs exploded more or less simultaneously on the Underground at about 08:50. These were:

In the third car of a C stock train between Liverpool Street and Aldgate at the approach to Aldgate Junction on an outer rail Circle line train.

In the second car of a C stock train immediately after leaving Edgware Road (subsurface) line station on an inner rail Circle line working, with damage another train which happened to be passing.

In the first car of a 1973 tube stock train, shortly after leaving King's Cross St Pancras on a southbound Piccadilly Line train towards Russell Square.

Initial thoughts at the Network Control Centre, supported by some of the reports which were coming in, were that there had been a massive power failure. Others had different views; the Group Station Manager at Edgware Road thought there might be somebody under a train, a train might have been derailed, or a train might have hit the tunnel walls.

• At 08:59 a call was made by the Network Control Centre to the London Fire Brigade and the London Ambulance Service to dispatch units to all three sites.

• At 09:15, a Code Amber alert on the Underground was declared, which meant that all trains, everywhere on the system, were to be evacuated and services suspended.

• At 09:47, a fourth bomb on the top deck of a route 30 bus exploded in Tavistock Square.

• At 10:00, the National Grid confirmed there were no power supply problems. Also at 10:00, most main-line termini were closed.

• At 11:08, bus services in Central London (Zone 1) were suspended, also DLR services from 11:15.

• At 15:25, main-line stations apart from King's Cross started to reopen, but all Underground services remained suspended for the rest of the day. Some DLR services were restored by 15:50. Buses withdrawn

Below: Hammersmith depot on the H&C line is very restricted, both in terms of space available and also the functions which can be carried out there. It is still essentially the original, as provided by the Great Western company. A train of C stock is entering the depot at the end of the morning peak on 9 April 2008; the tracks towards Paddington are on the left. John Glover

Right: *The old sidings at White City were in the type of accommodation which sadly does little credit to the railway. The conductor rail is of the long superseded type, but was still serviceable for the limited use to which it was put. This picture was taken shortly after the premises ceased to be used.* Author's collection

Right: *This is where trains leave the new White City sidings for the running lines, showing the back of a departing train of 1992 stock. Of note are the signalling arrangements and the well-defined walkway for staff. The track bed here and throughout the sidings is solid concrete slab.* Author's collection

from Zone 1 were restored by late evening, which did help people to get home.

The explosions took place at the time when the number of passengers travelling on the Underground peaks, between 08:45 and 09:00. Over 200,000 passengers would have been travelling on over 500 trains.

Recovery

On the following day, Friday 8 July, Underground services resumed, except:
* Circle and Hammersmith & City – No service.

* Edgware Rd – Wimbledon – No service north of High Street Kensington.
* Metropolitan – No service east of Baker Street.
* Piccadilly – No service east of Hyde Park Corner or south of Arnos Grove.
* King's Cross St Pancras Underground station remained closed for all services.

From Saturday 9 July, Metropolitan services were restored east of Baker Street, to terminate at Moorgate, and a three-train 15min Hammersmith & City service was restored between Hammersmith and Paddington only. Additional supporting bus services are not recorded here.

Six trains per hour go to Heathrow Terminals 1, 2, 3 via Terminal 4. These trains will wait at Heathrow Terminal 4 for up to eight minutes before continuing to Heathrow Terminals 1, 2, 3.

Going to central London?

There are 12 trains per hour from Heathrow Terminals 1, 2, 3, six trains per hour from Heathrow Terminal 4 and six trains per hour from Heathrow Terminal 5.

The journey time to Heathrow Terminals 1, 2, 3 from Cockfosters (83 mins) and from all other Piccadilly line stations en route e.g. Leicester Square (48 mins) or Hammersmith (31 mins) is given, from which the user deducts 1 min for Terminal 4 or adds 5 mins for Terminal 5.

However, what is not pointed out is that passengers bound for Terminals 1, 2, 3, finding that the next train goes to Terminal 4 first, may well get there more quickly by waiting for a Terminal 5 train which goes to Terminals 1, 2, 3 directly. There is no mention anywhere of the Rayners Lane/Uxbridge service.

The above demonstrates how complicated it can be to communicate such a service pattern to the public in an adequate but nevertheless precise manner.

It is difficult to beat an arrangement in which all stations are served in strict succession, ending with a rail terminal at or beyond which there is sufficient room provided for trains to layover as may be necessary to ensure that the timetable can be operated punctually.

Left: The Service Update boards have varied a little over time; this one shows the situation at 15:15 on Saturday 24 April 2004 with three partial suspensions for engineering work but no other out of course delays. John Glover

Below: Kensal Green station was one of those transferred to London Underground control when London Overground became the operator of the Euston–Watford dc services. A southbound Bakerloo Line train of 1972 Mk 2 stock pulls away on 26 April 2006. As is evident here, graffiti can be a serious problem. The West Coast Main Line can just be seen in the distance, to the right of the dc tracks. John Glover

Above: *The reconstruction of Wembley Park has enhanced its ability to accommodate large crowds. On the platforms there has also been much change. Seen here on 29 April 2009, the new bridge, for staff only, and the other station fittings. All are clearly in a modern style.* John Glover

Right: *Royal Oak on the Hammersmith & City is not the easiest of the surface stations to access. The one and only street entrance has this long stepped descent to the island platform and the elderly gentleman in this picture was clearly having difficulty. On the other hand, it is not one of the busiest stations on the system, and there have to be priorities for such matters.* John Glover

Next moves

It is no part of this book to suggest to what extent new terminals and/or a new runway should be built at Heathrow. However, serving new sites using an existing underground railway can cause severe difficulties, the practicalities of which one hopes will be fully considered as part of the decision on how (if at all) to proceed further. The problems of the Heathrow Express service, while different, are equally intractable.

White City development

The Shepherds Bush area underwent major railway works as a result of the construction of the very large Westfield Shopping Centre. London Underground is Westfield's partner, and the company acquired the freehold of the entire site for which the developer was granted a 203-year lease. London Underground is not directly funding any of the White City transport developments.

Sidings

There are two distinct elements. First was the opportunity to relocate the 16 sidings further west. That capacity was to be retained, and while it would be built on the surface, the whole would be covered over by the Westfield development and for which suitable supports would need to be built. It would thus be completely underground (and consequently subject to s12 Fire Regulations).

The stabling area is constructed with a track slab. There is no traditional ballast, anywhere. Each stabling position is fully signalled and all train movements within the sidings are normally made in the 'Coded Manual' mode. Each of the four groups of sidings has its own traction-current supply.

Each pair of siding roads is provided with an intermediate raised walkway, to give level access to and from all doors of stabled trains at all times. However, the benefits of a raised walkway as opposed to climbing up from ground level also bring the risk of personnel, mostly cleaners, falling off when there is no train present. Thus all are provided with guard rails throughout, with swing gates to align with the doors on the train. Lighting is controlled by remote sensors, which turn the lights off when no movement is detected.

The accommodation block incorporates two shafts that deliver fresh air into the sidings stabling area.

An essential part of the White City Sidings work was the positioning of the depot feeder line adjacent to the existing eastbound Central Line single track, where it is descending into deep tunnel. This required a new deck and piers for the bridge carrying the Hammersmith & City over both Wood Lane itself and the Central Line on a 52-degree skew. The new bridge, which had been built alongside, was slid into position during a four-day engineering possession of the H&C in 2005.

White City Sidings became operational on 15 January 2007. They are used mainly for overnight stabling rather than daytime storage, and can act as a bolt hole to aid service recovery. As sidings rather than a depot, they are part of the operational railway.

Wood Lane

A new station has been constructed on the Hammersmith & City Line and named Wood Lane. It is situated adjacent to the viaduct and is 250m south of White City station on the Central Line. Both are on the same side of the road. The Central Line tracks pass directly underneath the new station building in rafted-over cuttings.

The station entrance hall features the viaduct supports, and escalators lead to the two side platforms.

Left: *The Leslie Green style is evident in the Kentish Town Road entrance to Camden Town Northern Line station, seen on 1 June 2009. A second entrance is in Camden High Street, which backs onto this one. The station may seem likely to be big enough, but on Sunday afternoons it is available for interchange and exit only because of the crowds attending Camden Market. It is a key point in the Northern line geography, with branches north to High Barnet and Edgware, and south via Bank and via Charing Cross. One additional layer only of commercial development may be seen. John Glover*

Above: *The reversal of trains at turnback points can be a time-consuming business. Where there is merely a siding and no platform, as at Rayners Lane, the driver has to walk through the train, opening and shutting the connecting doers as he goes. How much better if the train could be left to carry out the manoeuvre without a driver? That is one possible outcome of the Piccadilly Line upgrade. A train of 1973 stock is seen here arriving from Rayners Lane from Uxbridge, siding centre, in February 2003. John Glover*

Right: *This is the westbound platform at Leyton, an unassuming former Great Eastern station. The columns mark the back of the main platform, as it were, providing an unenclosed but sheltered waiting area beyond it, with seats. It is 9 March 2009. John Glover*

Lifts are also provided. Each platform has full-length canopies to protect passengers from the weather.

Wood Lane station opened on 12 October 2008. The station on the H&C Line immediately to the south has been renamed Shepherd's Bush Market.

The existing Shepherd's Bush Central Line station was closed for eight months in 2008 to enable the escalators to be replaced and a new surface building to be constructed by Metronet BCV. This faces the entrance to the newly-opened Shepherd's Bush station on what is now the London Overground. A bus station has been built in the intervening area.

Victoria Line upgrade

Forty years after the Victoria Line opened, just about everything was worn out. That included the 1967-stock trains, the signalling, the power supplies and the track. The PPP foresaw new rolling stock, new signalling and journey time reductions.

The fleet of 39½ 1967 stock trains was later extended to 43 by the judicious conversion of some 1972 Mk 1 vehicles. The Victoria Line was the first to offer Automatic Train Operation (ATO). The original trains are in the course of being replaced by the 2009 stock, with which it is intended to run a 43-train service at the peak. They enter service in 2010.

A new line-control centre has been constructed at Northumberland Park and the 'Distance to Go' ATP signalling is being supplied by Westinghouse. This is a development of that already in use here. The simultaneous running of old and new stock, together with old signalling and new signalling is to be avoided, or your safety case becomes very difficult indeed!

The Victoria Line has two main distinguishing features. First, its 22km are entirely underground, save only for Northumberland Park depot. Thus there is nowhere on the line itself where materials can be stored before installation, or put until they can be cleared away for scrap or reuse. Each item has to be brought in to where it is wanted at the time it is wanted, and this usually means by train.

That is the second weakness, in that the only rail connections are those from the eastbound Piccadilly to the northbound Victoria, and from the southbound Victoria to the westbound Piccadilly, in both cases at Finsbury Park. This places severe constraints on the working of engineering trains, given that they have to reach Finsbury Park from Lillie Bridge or Ruislip in the first place, and it is not possible to replace sections of track over which trains need to be run until they have done so. Similarly, other tunnel work such as signalling is also limited, since it is not possible for workers to stand aside from the track while a train passes.

Trackwork

Project work on the Victoria Line track required an examination of the present asset condition, deciding on the scope of the work required, designing what needs to be done, acquiring the materials and scheduling the labour needed, and its installation within whatever constraints there may be. These include site access, and then testing and handover.

The aim was to get the track into good condition and then to keep it so without an undue amount of future attention. Eighty per cent of the track was found to need some work, as did 60% of the conductor rail. Other interested parties are those concerned with signalling and power supplies, as well as those wanting to test the new rolling stock. The track was mostly held in very good quality concrete, which thus took longer to break out. It soon became clear that access during engineering hours only would not be sufficient.

The choice was between closing the line early at 22:00 and weekend (or longer) closures. Some of the constraints are less obvious. Thus there can be no welding of rails before all passenger traffic ceases at stations shared with other lines, or it will set off the fire alarms. These need to be isolated first.

Croxley link

One of the odder results of past railway construction was the Metropolitan & Great Central Joint Watford branch of 1925, which never managed to reach Watford proper, as intended. To the south, the London & North Western Railway's branch from Watford Junction ended at its own less than satisfactory terminus of Croxley Green.

A scheme to link the two involves the building of 500m of new viaduct across the Grand Union Canal and the A412, the construction of a new station at Ascot Road, revamping the now closed Watford West station with two platforms, and electrification. Trains would then proceed to Watford High Street and Watford Junction stations. All Metropolitan line trains would be diverted to terminate there.

This long-running scheme seems to be generally supported in local government circles, but capital funding remains elusive. All the lines concerned are in Hertfordshire. What was once a modest £40m project has now risen in cost to around £150m.

At present, Watford Metropolitan station, which would be closed, sees 1.6m passengers annually (arrivals plus departures), rather more than most of the other LUL stations in the vicinity. Only Rickmansworth and Northwood, both with 1.9m, have more. A frequent all-day service of six trains per hour is offered even on Sundays, when usage is only a third of that during the week.

Those wanting to reach Watford High Street from, say, Harrow, would be better advised to take the present much more direct DC service from Harrow & Wealdstone. Journey time is 14 mins, compared with the Metropolitan's present 21 mins from Harrow-on-the-Hill to the present terminus, and perhaps four minutes more to Watford High Street.

Once funded, completion could be achieved in about five years.

Bending the Circle

The Circle Line was inherently unsatisfactory to operate; there are flat junctions everywhere to cause pathing delays, and virtually all parts of it are shared with other lines.

As a result, the Circle was unreliable and recent demand growth had caused station stop times and hence overall journey times to lengthen. Trains took longer to make the trip, which meant that more trains were in theory required, but without a terminal point service recovery is very difficult.

In practice, some journeys had to be missed due to trains running increasingly late.

None of this would be helped by the forthcoming removal of the reversing facility at Whitechapel, which was to be used for Crossrail construction; in consequence all Hammersmith & City trains need to continue to Plaistow or Barking.

There were also problems in that Wimbledon could do with more services to the City rather than Edgware

Road as a destination, the Hammersmith & City service needed bolstering, and more Metropolitan trains to Aldgate would be a good idea.

The total size of the C stock fleet which is based at Hammersmith and operates all the services mentioned (except those of the Metropolitan) is effectively fixed.

Subsurface lines upgrade

The subsurface lines upgrade will deliver 45% capacity increase in the central area, and the proposed service to be operated in 2018 will show considerable frequency gains nearly everywhere. Not least, these will be on the line to Hammersmith H&C.

However, the problems discussed are here now, and in any event the implementation of a brand new service pattern simultaneously with the upgrade poses its own risks.

It was therefore decided to make the service change on 13 December 2009, using the existing stock. This met many of the problems, and reliability should be improved.

The basic specification is that the long-running Circle line service is discontinued. It is replaced by a 'Circle' service running (both directions) Hammersmith – Edgware Road – Aldgate – High Street Kensington – Edgware Road.

This has the following consequences (off-peak services):

Layover time for Circle trains is available at both Hammersmith (three platforms) and Edgware Road (nominally Platform 2 only).

The reversing of the 6tph of the new Circle service is shared with the 6tph (H&C) at Hammersmith, and the 6tph (Wimbledon service) is confined to Platform 3 at Edgware Road. Platform occupancy, especially at Edgware Road and given the conflicting access movements, is thus tight.

All through services between Paddington and the City depart from the present H&C platforms at Paddington.

National Rail passengers at Paddington 'need to be educated' to go to the right platforms.

Hammersmith & City and Circle trains are both reduced in frequency from 7.5tph to 6tph.

Trains reversing at Whitechapel H&C are extended to Plaistow.

The combined service provision from Hammersmith through to Edgware Road is nearly doubled in frequency from 7.5tph to 12tph.

All Circle Line passengers whose previous journey took them through Edgware Road need to change trains there, and for many of them that means crossing the footbridge.

Operationally, the section between Praed St Junction (where the H&C leaves the Circle/Wimbledon service) and Edgware Road (about 300m) has become very busy indeed!

High Street Kensington–Olympia District services are reduced from 4tph to 3tph.

The new service pattern represents a brave attempt to redistribute existing resources to meet passenger requirements more effectively, though there are as indicated some losers as well as the rather more numerous passengers who gain. It is, though, an intermediate stage in the line upgrade programme.

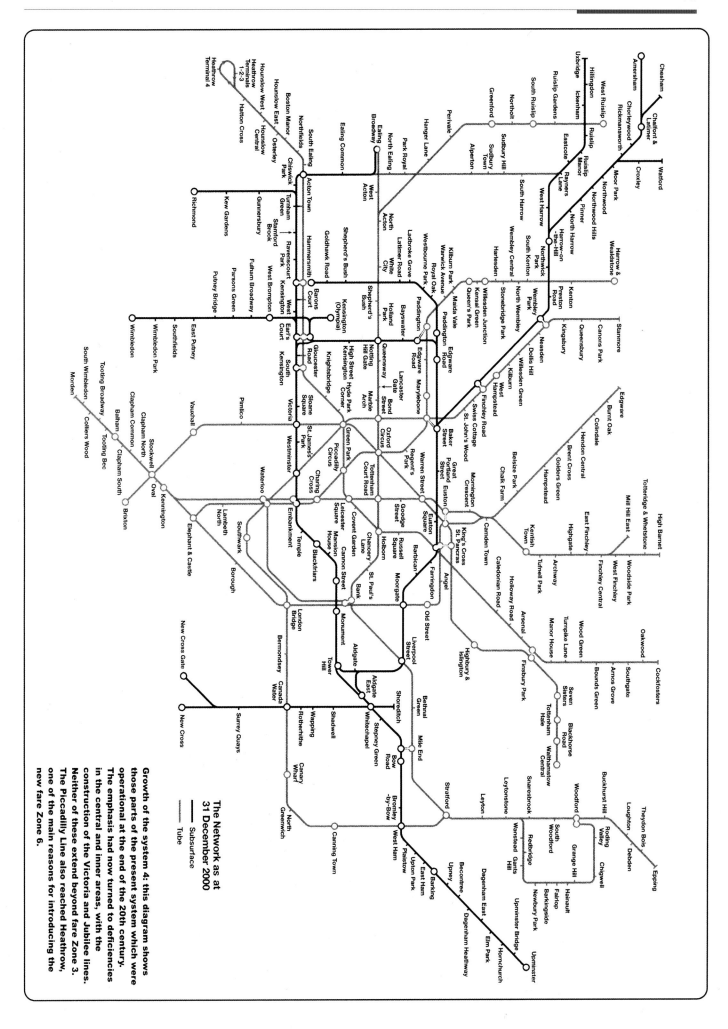

**The Network as at
31 December 2000**

—— Subsurface

—— Tube

Growth of the system 4: this diagram shows
those parts of the present system which were
operational at the end of the 20th century.
The emphasis had now turned to deficiencies
in the central and inner areas, with the
construction of the Victoria and Jubilee lines.
Neither of these extend beyond fare Zone 3.
The Piccadilly Line also reached Heathrow,
one of the main reasons for introducing the
new fare Zone 6.

11

A CHALLENGING FUTURE

The benefits of a Decently Modern Metro, or whatever the catchphrase of the moment may be, are nowadays rather clearer than they once were. It would seem that London, like other world cities, has come to terms with the need for the substantial injection of public funds on a long-term basis. This is particularly the case for capital expenditure. The benefits of the Underground to the city as a whole are considerably more than those which could be realised by London Underground in purely commercial terms.

An example of this is the Jubilee Line, for which a 2004 study demonstrated that building Canary Wharf station alone had added £2bn to land values in the area – or over half the costs of constructing the entire line. Similarly, Southwark station had provided local landowners with an £0.8bn bonus.

Social pricing

There are other factors at work, too. The pricing of travel is set at levels which are attractive to the passenger, and the would-be passenger. Thus in 2009 fares reductions on the Underground were granted to all children aged 11 to 15 carrying a 11–15 Oyster photocard (free for under 11s), also 16–19 year olds who live in London and are in full-time education or similar. Here, a 16+ Oyster photocard is needed. Holders of New Deal photocards can also get reduced rate fares, and season tickets are available at discount rates to certain groups. Discounts are also available to holders of some National Rail Railcards. Finally, residents of London boroughs who are aged 60 or over have free travel on the Underground at all times, as do disabled people of any age.

Above: *This view of the subsurface lines at Farringdon and featuring an A stock train on a westbound service shows the reverse curve of the formation and hence the platforms at this location. This is not an impossible problem at such a degree of curvature, but it still produces a much larger train to platform gap than would be the case if the platforms were straight. It is 29 April 2009. John Glover*

Left: *The London 2012 Games will see considerable use made of West Ham station for spectator access. Before 1979, the only rail service at West Ham in recent times was the District/Hammersmith & City operation. Now c2c trains stop here, as does the Jubilee. From the westbound Jubilee line platform, the new Docklands Light Railway station replacing the North London Line service is taking shape on 23 July 2009. The DLR will provide additional railway capacity between Canning Town and Stratford. John Glover*

A CHALLENGING FUTURE

Above: *The Grand Union Canal viaduct is crossed by the Metropolitan's Watford branch less than a kilometre before reaching its terminus. The new route to Watford (High Street and Junction) will need to leave the existing railway before this point, and a new bridge will be built over the canal. A train of A stock crosses the Grand Union on 14 September 2008.* John Glover

Little of this can be regarded as commercial pricing; it comes more under the heading of social benefits, and the operator needs to be compensated accordingly. Shortfalls in operator fares income for these reasons should not have to be made good out of a transport budget.

Pricing of this nature will also, no doubt, have helped to drive up the volume of travel.

As far as costs are concerned, management has to ensure that the unit costs of operations, particularly labour costs, are kept under continuous scrutiny and are not allowed to spiral out of control.

Growth pressures

A lot of the need for the large-scale PPP works on updating the Underground are based on the need to accommodate recent growth. Just how substantial have these been? The overall levels of Underground traffic in the years following World War 2, as measured by the number of journeys made on the system, are shown in Table 11.1:

Table 11.1: Passenger journeys on London Underground, selected years.

Year	Passenger journeys (millions)	As index (1949=100)
1949	641	100
1954	671	105
1959	669	104
1964	674	105
1969	675	105
1974	636	99
1979	594	93
1982	498	78
1984	651	102
1988/89	815	127
1993/94	735	115
1998/99	866	136
2003/04	948	148
2008/09	1,089	170

Table 11.1 shows how a plateau was reached in the 1950s and 1960s, after which volumes slowly declined. The opening of the Victoria Line (1968–72) seems to have had a negligible effect on the total numbers carried; presumably they would have been that much fewer without it. The nadir was 1982, which followed the Fares Fair episode when an overnight doubling of fares took place.

More passengers

With the more stable regime which followed, together with the introduction of Travelcard, passenger journeys began what was to become a sustained volume of growth. The economic downturn in the early 1990s was a setback, but this proved to be only temporary.

Table 11.1 illustrates how slow decline has turned to near-continuous growth, and why some of the economy measures of earlier years were made. Some of the growth could be catered for by using that discarded capacity, but it is a salutary thought that today more than twice the numbers of passengers are now being carried on London Underground than in 1982. In that period, the Jubilee Line and the Heathrow T4 and T5 extensions of the Piccadilly Line have been added to the network, Wood Lane has opened, and the gain of the Waterloo & City from British Rail has been offset by the loss of the East London to London Overground. There has also been a transfer of some stations from Silverlink to London Underground, but service patterns have remained stable.

Passenger journeys are of course not the only measure, but the average journey length of about 8km has stayed remarkably constant over the years. By definition, passengers from National Rail who use only the Waterloo & City line (2.4km long) have shorter journeys, and commuters from Amersham, Cockfosters or Epping will travel rather further.

Ten-Year Business Plan

This plan was launched by the London Mayor, Boris Johnson, in November 2008. It covers the years to 2017/18. For the Underground, it focuses on the upgrade works, including the supporting of the 2012 Games. Priorities include the expansion of capacity, completing the transformation of the Tube, the delivery of new air-conditioned trains, improved reliability and faster journeys.

By 2012, the TfL Business Plan forecasts that the first of the large-scale Tube upgrades on the Jubilee, Victoria and Northern Lines will have been delivered, each providing between 20 and 30 per cent more capacity into central London, and early batches of the first ever air-conditioned trains on the subsurface lines.

By 2018, the remaining upgrades on the Piccadilly, the District, Circle, Hammersmith & City and Metropolitan Lines will also be finished, providing a 28% increase in Underground capacity. Further works will follow on the Northern and Bakerloo.

There will be further schemes to cool deeper tube lines, and major improvements at Bond Street, Paddington, Tottenham Court Road and Victoria stations.

For the Underground, the 2012 Games require that the planned completion of the upgrade works on the Central, Jubilee and Northern lines are achieved. This includes the construction at Stratford of an additional westbound Central Line platform, and new pedestrian bridges both here and at West Ham.

Left: *The 2012 London Games will be in its way a test for the whole country in terms of carrying them off successfully. Transport provision will play a large part in this, whether for the so-called 'Olympic Family' or the spectators. This shows the new second platform for the westbound Central Line trains being installed at Stratford on 9 March 2009. It is when people leave the arenas, all at much the same time, that is likely to cause the most problems. Arrivals before the events will be more staggered.*
John Glover

Investment programme

It is worth recording that projects to be included in the investment programme have to meet the following generally unexceptional criteria:
- Is it deliverable within the stated cost, time and performance criteria?
- Is it affordable, in terms of both total expected expenditure and the associated risks?
- Does it offer value for money in terms of whole-life cost and fitness for purpose, and meet users' requirements?
- Will the results contribute to TfL's overall strategy?

Future projections

The future situation depends to a substantial extent on factors way outside the control of London Underground.

For instance, projections to 2025, which is only 15 years or so away, suggest that by then the London population will have risen roundly 10% from 7.5m in 2006 to 8.3m by then. The number of jobs will have increased rather faster, from 4.6m jobs in 2006 to 5.45m in 2026, or by 18%. Both are intrinsically related to housing policies in terms of where these people will live, where the jobs will be created, and the means used to link one with the other. Land use is all-important.

The first need is to get the most out of what is already there, and this is the aim of the present upgrades. Service quality and reliability are part of the equation, as are accessibility, safety and security. Service integration between the various modes also has scope for improvement.

Opposite top: West Hampstead is a difficult location, with three stations. These are for the Jubilee line (here) and on the other side of the road for the North London and then for Thameslink. There is none for Chiltern Railways, but should (or could) there be? The range of connections which would become available would be huge. This view of August 2004 from the Jubilee platforms shows, beyond the northbound Metropolitan, where platforms for the two Chiltern tracks would need to be. Draft plans would see the stations for all four lines united within a single pedestrianised area.
John Glover

Opposite bottom: The close proximity of the District and National Rail at Bromley-by-Bow (and for the next 20km to Upminster) also sees two railways, owned by different organisations, with totally different electrification systems, running side by side. How safe is that, for the staff of either, working on the track? Here grandfather rights apply, but this could have been a real problem had one of the western Crossrail branches have gone to Aylesbury as intended in the 1990s scheme. An eastbound D stock train arrives at Bromley-by-Bow in June 2003. Even the overhead masts span the Underground tracks here. John Glover

Pinch points

Beyond that, new capacity will be required, by London Underground or other forms of railway. These include the East London Line extension (opening from 2010), Thameslink and Crossrail. Both the latter are under construction.

It should also be borne in mind that the situation will vary at different times of the day, days of the week or seasons of the year.

Thus from time to time Wembley Park station can take on an altogether different aspect from that of a busy suburban centre. West End stations are busy late at night. Commuter traffic drops off generally during the summer holiday period, but this is also the main tourist season, which is a separate market with rather different travel requirements.

The following sections of line have been identified as likely to be the Underground's most crowded in 2026:

Central	Bank–Bethnal Green
District	Parsons Green–Earl's Court
Jubilee	London Bridge–Canary Wharf
Northern	Euston–Angel, also Clapham South–London Bridge
Piccadilly	Arsenal–Holborn
Victoria	Highbury & Islington–Oxford Circus, also Victoria–Green Park

How these problem areas might be addressed is another matter, and it may be noted that the long-talked about Chelsea–Hackney line, in whatever form it might take in terms of tube, subsurface or even main-line type operation, would only bring relief to some of these areas. The presently proposed route of this scheme (Epping to Wimbledon via King's Cross St Pancras, Tottenham Court Road, Piccadilly Circus and Victoria) is safeguarded.

Conclusion

London Underground now faces a future as challenging as any it has faced in its century and a half of history. Tim O'Toole, London Underground's Managing Director from 2003 to 2009, sums up the situation as he saw it at the end of his distinguished period of office:

"We have hit new heights, carrying more people and delivering more service than ever before.

"The renewal and expansion of the public transport network will play a crucial role in leading economic recovery, enabling people to get to and from work and allowing them to move around the city for leisure and social activities.

"We must put right decades of under-investment and accomplish over the next 15 years what should have been done over the last 50.

"Without our upgrade programme, London would face a future with ever-increasing transport congestion and declining reliability. We are now building the modern, efficient and integrated system that London needs and deserves."

Opposite top: *A train of the 1928 District line stock sits at Wimbledon with its doors open on 25 May 1963 ready to form a service for Edgware Road. These trains now look very dated; will vehicles in the present fleets age in just the same way? Perhaps this train would look better in Underground corporate livery? One might hope that the designer's art has improved over the years.* Electrail Collection (4406)

Opposite bottom: *Swansong for the A stock; a standard 8-car formation arrives at Hillingdon, crossing the A40(M) bridge as it does so on 28 June 2008. This is not a formal park-and-ride station, but it is well connected by road and clearly has many users who park there for the day.* John Glover

Left: *The bay platform at Chalfont & Latimer on the Metropolitan Line is presently used by the Chesham shuttle, but as can be seen in this view of 14 September 2008 its length is quite limited. Extending further behind the photographer to cater for longer trains would end up blocking the entrance to the car park. Extending parallel to the southbound line would mean knocking down the station buildings and probably making that platform accessible only by subway. An arriving train of A stock from Amersham is seen in the distance.* John Glover

References and Bibliography

This book has evolved through many editions, and the sources of much of the information are uncertain after so many years. On more recent topics, searching the web and starting with the Transport for London website has much to commend it. For secondary sources, though, a check on any information derived is highly desirable.

The Annual Report and Accounts of London Transport, in whatever form that body has taken over the years, are good base documents. Similarly, the Department for Transport's annual volume Transport Statistics.

The standard work on London Transport is still T. C. Barker and Michael Robbins' A History of London Transport. Volume 1 The Nineteenth Century (1963), and Volume 2 The Twentieth Century to 1970 (1974), both Allen & Unwin. For more detail on individual lines, the series of volumes by various authors and published by Capital Transport can be recommended.

Dealing specifically with the Underground, the technical side of the rolling stock is dealt with in loving detail by J. Graeme Bruce in three complementary volumes: Steam to Silver (Capital Transport, 1983), The London Underground Tube Stock (Ian Allan, 1988), and Workhorses of the London Underground (Capital

Transport, 1987). My own London Underground Rolling Stock in Colour for the Modeller and Historian (Ian Allan Publishing, 2009) is a wide ranging and largely photographic offering, while my similarly titled book on London Underground Stations (Ian Allan Publishing, 2009) is a companion volume. For what makes it happen, try the present author's Principles of London Underground Operations (Ian Allan Publishing, 2000). Fleet details will be found in Brian Hardy's London Underground Rolling Stock, (Capital Transport, 15th edition, 2002).

Douglas Rose's splendidly detailed and privately published The London Underground: A Diagrammatic History (8th edition, December 2007), knows no equal. For detailed line by line drawings, Railway Track Diagrams 5: Southern & TfL (3rd edition 2008) published by TRACKmaps for the Quail Map Co is most valuable.

Of the company histories, few can compare with Alan A. Jackson's London's Metropolitan Railway, (David & Charles, 1986). Also from Alan A. Jackson, in conjunction with Desmond Croome, comes Rails Through the Clay, 2nd edition, 1994.

Underground-related articles appear from time to time in Modern Railways, Railway Gazette International and other magazines. Finally, Underground News, the monthly journal of the London Underground Railway Society, can be recommended.

Below: The problem with the 1959 stock was the lack of anything which could be called luggage space, and the necessity of providing something for airport services. Thus the 1973 stock offered greater standbacks at the doors, which could perform a dual function. This view is of a refurbished unit at Cockfosters on 10 April 2008, showing further rearrangements with some seating losses. John Glover